Kingdom Ops

A Next Level Shift, Vol. IV.

GIRL, GET YOUR FIGHT BACK!

Finish Strong Anointing!

PRESENTER: TRINA D. WELLS

© Copyright 2019 - All rights reserved.

The content contained within this book may not be reproduced, duplicated or transmitted without direct written permission from the author or the publisher.

Under no circumstances will any blame or legal responsibility be held against the publisher, or author, for any damages, reparation, or monetary loss due to the information contained within this book, either directly or indirectly.

Disclaimer Notice:

Please note the information contained within this document is for educational and entertainment purposes only. All effort has been executed to present accurate, up to date, reliable, complete information.

No warranties of any kind are declared or implied. Readers acknowledge that the author is not engaged in the rendering of legal, financial, medical or professional advice. The content within this book has been derived from various sources. Please consult a licensed professional before attempting any techniques outlined in this book.

Table of Contents

Chapter One: Upgrade ~Shift~ Level Up 1

Satina Grissom 1

Chapter Two: The Payne, Purpose, Purge & Praise. Season Of Self-Identification 10

Jacquaye A. Payne 10

Chapter Three: Keep Hanging On, The Breaking Is For The Making! 26

Shonquil Jones-Dyson 26

Chapter Four: Know When And Know How 37

Dr. Cynthia J. Hines 37

Chapter Five: The Blessing In My Brokenness 50

Gricelda R. Ramsey 50

Chapter Six: I Lost Some Battles But I Won The War 63

Monsenaray Sheppard 63

Chapter Seven: "Undisputed" 74

Kibra Vanhorn 74

Chapter Eight: It's A Faith Fight.....Fighting To The Finish........... 87

Cassonya Carter 87

Chapter Nine: " The Silence " 105

Kenshalene Minott 105

Chapter Ten: "Be Fabulous & Forgive" 117

Apollonia Ellis 117

Chapter Eleven: Why Me? Why Not You? 129

Brucina L. Mayfield 129

Chapter Twelve: War Room Notes 141

Nakia Moody 141

Chapter Thirteen: "Just Before Dawn" 157

Trina D. Wells 157

Chapter One

Upgrade ~Shift~ Level Up

Satina Grissom

My Appearance

My appearance was always together, hair fried, dyed and laid to the side; outfits cute and all put together, but I was broken. Broken from an abortion, broken from word curses that stuck to me like crazy glue. My self-esteem was pretty much a mound of dust with a few lumps mingled in between of what used to be my identity. GOD… HELP ME!

Where was I to go? Who could help me or how could I help myself? I prayed to God daily, but in my heart, I felt nothing. Even as I write this chapter, I'm overcome with tears because I never realized what a bad place I was in mentally and spiritually, until this very moment. I knew that somehow God would send help to deliver me or

I'd find myself in a mental hospital only to be diagnosed as a functioning manic-depressive. As I recall sitting in the middle of my bed, literally crying out to God to save my mind and to heal my brokenness, nothing changed, not immediately anyway. I was looking for God to be a magician and magically transport me to the greater.

The transformation that began to take place in my life took years of progression. The process began when I opened my mouth and asked God to forgive me and to heal every area of my life that was broken and in disarray. That is when I decided to participate in the book collaboration,

Volume I of A Next Level Shift: Kingdom Upgrade. Through that opportunity I was able to share my story, to free my mind and expose the enemies that were taunting me.

Pushing through many tears, loads of frustration, a gazillion of why's and when's, I stayed in a posture of emptying and receiving. Boy was that hard. I wanted so badly to go back to the place that had broken and pushed me to the arms of God because it was familiar. I knew that going back would only position me between a rock and hell.

Why I Write

When I started writing I was afraid of the memories and the pain that would resurface, not to mention the trauma that it had left embedded in my heart. Not only would writing leave me totally transparent, but it would also leave me to be ridiculed… then I realized, people were already doing that.

Writing my story pushed me through a press. The best analogy I will use is this: Imagine a tube of toothpaste. In order to get all the toothpaste out of the tube, you must first squeeze from the bottom and roll the tube up as you go. The more you do this, the better chance you'll have at getting all the toothpaste out as it empties. If you don't properly squeeze the tube and roll up as you go, you leave so much toothpaste (residue) inside of the tube because you didn't properly dispense of the toothpaste. I said that to say, God was properly dispensing me in every way possible in order to not leave any traces of residue behind.

Writing was a major tool that helped change my life in a major way. Through these writing collaborations my life has changed tremendously. Through every "Upgrade", God had brought about a shift in my life that has caused me to level up in God. I understand what my grandmother meant when she said, "Every round goes higher and higher." It really does and it's marvelous in my eyes (Psalm 118:2). Three years ago, no one could have told me that today I would be the assistant praise and worship leader of my local church, I lead intercessory prayer on Sundays, I have been afforded the opportunity to produce two skits for Women of the Bible for the Aglow Ministries of Muskegon, only to later present at their international conference on Mackinaw Island and as of May 2019, I've been blessed to own and operate my very daycare/learning center, "Tina-Tots."

The Upgrade

I'm beyond humbled for where God has taken me and from where he's delivered me. Not for one split second, do or have, I ever thought I've arrived. The upgrade in my life has been apparent and visible, but it has come with a price. A price of many tears, a lot of sacrifices and the separation of relationships. I am reminded of the song "*Yes*" by Shekinah Glory Ministries, where the leader of the song says, "*Be careful when telling God Yes, because Yes may cost you everything,*" and to a certain extent, it did.

When God begins to upgrade you, be advised, that you can't carry some things or people from the past with you. Your upgrade is for you, not them. Let me repeat that, the upgrade is for you, not them, so don't be surprised when your path from people, places and things began to take a different course. The Bible states in Romans 12:2, "And be not conformed to this world, but be ye transformed by the renewing of your mind that ye may prove what is that good and acceptable and perfect will of God." The upgrade begins in your mind. It all starts with a thought.

Proverbs 23:7 states, "For as he thinketh in his heart so is he…" When God began to redefine who I was, he started with my thinking and the thoughts I had towards myself. He promoted my thoughts to seeing me the way he saw me. Scriptures that I'd heard all-too-often and took for granted, now had a different meaning. Scriptures like Deuteronomy 28:13 told me that I'm the head and not the tail; Psalm 17:8, "Keep me as the apple of your eye…" and finally, Psalm 138:8, "What concerns God, concerns me." These scriptures helped to upgrade my thinking.

During this time, I have discovered a new me. Like the former first lady of the United States Michelle Obama, entitled her book, "Becoming Michelle Obama." I'm becoming the Satina God created me to be.

The Shift

Now that the upgrade had begun to take place, there was no need of me remaining in the place of Lo-debar; that place that housed fear, doubt, resentment, rejection, etc., but how was I to get from Lo-debar... what was I to do? Shift. Shift? Yes Shift! Shift means to move from one place to another. Although I was not physically moving, I was spiritually moving to a different location. We all have moved at some point in our lives and we know that moving of any form is never easy. We all dread the packing and unpacking because we never realize how much we have accumulated over the years. His stuff, her stuff, children stuff, grand's stuff, on top of your stuff, until we start to sort through those things we've started to pack.

When it's time to move and unpack in the new location that is where we realize that the "stuff" we brought from the old location is no longer relevant to the new location. The Bible says in Mark 2:22, "No man puts new wine into old wine bottles; else the new wine burst the bottles and the wine is spilled and the bottles will be marred: but new wine must be put into new wine bottles." It is imperative that old baggage from the past be left behind. Listen, I believe Erykah Badu had a revelation when she wrote the song, "Bag Lady." The lyrics say, "Bag lady you gone hurt your back, dragging all them bags like that. I guess nobody ever told you, that all you must hold onto is you." Wooha! That right there was "shob". Drop all those bags that don't belong to you and SHIFT!!! Stop picking up other people's issue; they are not your issues to carry.

Level Up

When I finally started to surrender to God, old things began to pass away and my life began to come into alignment. God began to allow me to level up. I was now beginning to do things that I always desired in my heart. Things like speaking engagements, sharing my story, helping in the ministry, encouraging others, to now having my own business. If I had done any of these things prematurely, I would have forfeited my assignments and possibly wounded people along the way.

I read a quote, (author unknown) that said, *"If you don't heal from what hurt you, you'll bleed on people who didn't cut you."* The more I see my progress, the more I understand how important it was for me to get delivered and free from the things and people that had me bound before God could start elevating my life. Leveling up by no means, means that I have it all together or that I'm sitting on top of the world. It only means that I resisted my will and surrendered to the will of God for my life. Everyday is a day to level up, it's never an opportunity to think that I can take a break or fall back into an old mindset. No. It's an everyday goal to press toward the mark that God has laid before me.

When I look back over my life, today I have so much more to lose. You see, at one point I just wanted to be in God's will, my attitude was "whatever will be will be", but it's now much more important for me to be in his perfect will. When I started to align my will to God's will, that's when change took place. Lol… I'm always in agreement with his will, but since he sees all and knows all, I guess it's best that I follow suite. Obedience is better than sacrifice and I've sacrificed more than my share.

Some years ago, one of our co-authors, Anna Crockett, from Girl Get Your Fight Back said to me, "What's coming is better than what was." I did not see it then and I didn't understand what she meant, but I now understand it better by and by.

My friend, don't let baggage from your past weigh you down. Stop carrying things that were only meant to be used as steppingstones to get you to your next level. Everything that's in your heart to accomplish is yours to achieve. God put those desires inside of you. You will not fail. Don't let your dreams die. Girl, keep your faith and fight.

CHAPTER TWO

THE PAYNE, PURPOSE, PURGE & PRAISE. SEASON OF SELF-IDENTIFICATION

JACQUAYE A. PAYNE

The Payne

On January 1st, the new year came in as any other day. The thought of 2019 didn't bring about great optimism for the heights I'd soar nor pessimism for the woes-of-life I'd encounter. I did expect growth and understanding to come about because, if nothing else, I had learned how to keep pushing forward; past discomfort, struggles and doubt, all to shift into my next level.

Backing up a bit, 2018 ended a bit rocky as my oldest sister passed away of cancer at the age of 44. Her funeral, held on November 10, gave way for the first (and last) time that all seven of my biological siblings were under one roof at the same time. Unfortunately, one of the siblings was absent from the body, but there was a slight sense of comfort in knowing that after 28 years of waiting (the age of the youngest brother), we were able to finally share in that moment with one another, if nothing but for those few short hours during the funeral service.

Fast forward, once again, to the present moment: Today as I sit and analyze, I can assuredly say that I've been able to pinpoint the times in which I experienced issues of self-identity; periods of time when I knew who I was at that moment was not aligning with whom I knew God had called me to be.

A different type of nudging for self-identity and belonging had begun to burn within me once my siblings and I found out about my sister's diagnosis in early 2018. It was May, on my birthday in fact, which actually marked another first for the siblings; the first time that six of the seven of us were able to actually orchestrate a conversation over-the-phone with one another. This may not seem like a big deal to some, but to have never had the opportunity or know-how on where to even begin building relationships that life's many circumstances robbed us of, at no fault of our own, this moment was huge!

The condition of my sisters health was gently woven into the conversation after hours of gleeful laughs, jokes, and random trips down memory lane. We'd stayed on the phone all night and my other sister, a registered nurse, reminded the oldest that she had to get some rest before her first chemo/radiation treatment in the morning. At that point, thoughts of urgency crowded my mind, wondering how much time the siblings would have with one another and the likelihood of us being able to reconnect and make up for lost times which came as a direct result of a drug-addicted mother, multiple absentee fathers, hundreds of miles of distance between residences, and an almost two-decade prison sentence of my oldest brother when he was just a teenager.

The likelihood of getting all of the siblings together to share in a bonding experience that often comes naturally to brothers and sisters was feeling more and more unlikely; in fact, slim to none; especially with the one brother incarcerated in New Jersey, one brother living in Philadelphia, four siblings in Cleveland and me in Michigan. I couldn't help but envision what life could have been like if we were raised in the same household; if I'd been able to talk to my older sisters about how to value myself as a young lady or how protective my brothers would've been at the mention of my first date or first kiss.

So how did this unexpected sibling reunification phone call take shape? It all started from one brother calling with birthday wishes for me and my twin, thus beginning a ripple effect of one sibling calling the next on three-way and so on. Full confession, we can all be charged as guilty for dodging one another's phone calls from time-to-time, so this time seemed epic as we all willingly, yet unknowingly, committed to answering. We certainly didn't expect everyone who could, to connect and answer their phones, but God knows what you need when you need it.

To sum up that moment, that phone call gave us a feeling of comradery and closeness that we'd not experienced before then, although we had many life experiences as seasoned adults in our 20's, 30's and 40's… although just a phone conversation, it meant so much more to us! We always knew about one another, but the distance in proximity, perhaps abandonment issues resulting from negligent parents, and hesitation to connect as we got older grew year-by-year, as we had no solid foundation or parental guidance to draw from. That moment represented the beginning of the end, the beginning of new, openness and closure all at the same time.

The Purpose

By early January 2019, I'd been able to identify clear chunks of time in my life that shaped me into the woman I was, as in, the standards I'd upheld and the situations I'd settled for. Again, that self-identity piece. I remember shortly after my daughter being born in 2007, identifying how impacted I was by not having a father in my life to raise me when I saw my newborn daughter being held in her biological father's arms. Turns out, I had major daddy issues that I didn't even know existed. This set of issues ultimately shaped the treatment I accepted from men who I thought could fill an unidentified, missing void.

Upon the news of my sister's cancer diagnosis in May 2018 until my sister's passing that November, for the first time, I was able to acknowledge and understand how impacted I was by not being raised by our biological mother and the toll of being separated from my siblings had taken on me. I was an adulting woman, wife, mother, professional, author, friend, advocate and mentor… who had almost-debilitating separation issues (on top of the other set of daddy issues I previously referenced). I had only allowed myself to get comfortable or close to someone to a certain point, and never without my guard up, ready to flee and disconnect at a moments notice, if necessary.

I'd even considered the ramifications of not fully knowing who I was; my roots, and being able to pass on genealogy to my children as I was never quite sure who my father was and toggled around with getting a DNA test (this was important in the natural, but also in the spiritual as there's a need to know and identify generational blessings *and* curses attached to your bloodline as well).

So, I'd been dealing with all these emotions and thoughts for some months and I wasn't quite sure if we'd be doing another book collaboration (I'd previously participated in the first three volumes). I contemplated, however, if we were going to do another volume, what else I'd have to share. Afterall, I'd already poured out my testimony when I'd experienced a miserable marriage and survived, doubted myself for years and overcame, wore a facade and used jokes to cope with my pain, but came through that; how I initially believed the manipulation tactics and lies that I was ugly and disgusting, but realized they were indeed lies; how I'd invested so much into my education because it was something I could control, but I was too afraid to let God take control of my life, and so on. I literally had poured out and spoken out about everything I had to give in order to inspire others… so I thought.

The Purge

Back to that early January 2019 self-identification moment. Well, early in the morning on January 14, I was sitting and scrolling through my social media timeline (pause: It's critical that this isn't the first thing we allow to consume our mind in the morning as it is definitely so easy to do, but make sure that you're giving God His time as David tells us in **Psalm 63:1** (KJV), "...O God, You are my God; Early will I seek You; My soul thirsts for You; My flesh longs for You In a dry and thirsty land where there is no water").

While scrolling, I came across a video and when I clicked on it, it was of a 30+ year-old-woman explaining how she'd looked back over her life at her current age and questioned how she'd even become pregnant at 17 as a result of rape. She stated that she'd come from a good two-parent home; she was from a middle-class, well educated family, but with all that, she'd been raped, bore a child and almost 20 years later, was wondering how had she ended up in that particular situation.

I instantly paused in that very moment, set my phone down, and much like the words that appear in closed-caption on a tv screen, the words, "Was what I experienced considered molestation" flashed before my eyes. To this day, I am not fully sure why her words, right then and there, resonated, only to awaken and uncover a deeply embedded truth/secret within.

Can I be honest and tell you that at that moment, I was shaken and nervous to my core when considering the answer to my previously stated question; nervous of the answer that might arise if I actually took the time to dig deep within self *and* look up the definition of such a nasty word- molestation. I gave myself a brief pep talk, "JacQuaye, you are no longer eight-year-old-you and you were never weak because of things that happened beyond your control ... take a deep breath and Google the definition!" I did just that and for the first time in my adult life, I accepted that I was indeed molested and that I'd suppressed these encounters for the last 25 years of my life!

Right then and there, I knew that God was purging me of some deeply rooted issues, deeper than I ever thought was within me! I'd heard other people talk about molestation and rape before, sharing their testimonies, even as I'd been a part of the last three book collaboartions. I'd heard other authors talk about deliverance from sexual traumas they'd experienced, but nothing ever triggered a thought in me. Heck, on occasion I'd even spoken about the sexual trauma that other family members experienced as children growing up in my family, but I never saw myself as having that particular testimony nor that message of survival, because I'd buried the memories so deeply within myself; my own memories were hidden from even me!

That's is often the unintentional consequence of experiencing trauma; whether at a young age or older. Suppression is a real thing and can ultimately shape life-decisions, outcomes, victories or defeats in our lives. Suppression is described as follows:

Suppression noun

the conscious intentional exclusion from consciousness of a thought or feeling

We've all heard of the term, "Fight or Flight" (the instinctive physiological response to a threatening situation, which readies one either to resist forcibly or to run away). I'd classify suppression as a form of "flight" in which a part of you sort of, runs away and checks out of reality. Maybe the reality is too painful or harmful to add to your memory reservoir, so you simply exclude that chunk of time from your life as a survival mechanism.

On the flip side, when I questioned what else I had to pour out in order to include my writings in the next volume, I had no idea that I needed to be purged; purged of inner-filth and inner-guilt that laid dormant for all the prior years, all while taking a catastrophic hold over my life! By definition, to purge is described as follows:

Purge verb

To clear of guilt

To free from moral or ceremonial defilement to make free of something unwanted

I had been defiled and had things happen to me that I absolutely did not want or agree to! As an eight-year-old or 10-year-old, I could not have consented or given permission to anyone to violate me, put their hands on me, thrust their manly body parts upon my underdeveloped female anatomy. As an unwanted consequence, I held onto the shame of knowing that these males had done crud acts towards me.

And I carried the shame; shame of lying to those who raised me when they'd give me the usual, "You know you can tell me if something is wrong/Has anyone touched you/No means no," speeches, affirming that I could tell them if I was in danger. My inner-voice screamed "YES, I am being violated", but the mumblings of my mouth assured them that I was safe as I repeatedly lied and said that everything was okay.

The next set of shame came from knowing, even as early as eight-years-old, that if I didn't speak up about family members who were inappropriately engaging in behaviors with me, how many more cousins or children were also being impacted/touched because I did not speak up and tell the truth. So shame in being a coward was an ever-prevailing thought… and the guilt that if something happened to someone else, it would be all my fault was crippling (as a child, it's difficult to internalize that others actions are not predicated upon you; people make choices and their choices are just that- theirs).

And as the years passed and shame and guilt cloaked me like a blanket (not just any blanket by-the-way, but more like a Snuggie as it molds and contours to the shape of your body), this harmful truth became a part of my being; so when people looked at me, they didn't see the ill-fitting disaster within. They only saw the outward smiles, happy exterior and facade I wore on my face. They saw me excelling in school and in my extracurricular activities. They saw me as a happy, busy person; not as the person who was overcompensating for the internal damages and scars I carried within.

And I tried to believe that I was happy as well, all while knowing and feeling as if pieces of me had been robbed and stolen, but never knowing how to identify where those voids had come from because of how deeply things were hidden within. I didn't realize that a purge from those strongholds was necessary.

2 Corinthians 10:4-5 (KJV)- 4 (For the weapons of our warfare [are] not carnal, but mighty through God to the pulling down of strong holds;) 5 Casting down imaginations, and every high thing that exalteth itself against the knowledge of God, and bringing into captivity every thought to the obedience of Christ;

As I stated, certain occurrences in my recent life have triggered moments of recollection, from my sister's death to watching a video about rape, and caused me to be brutally honest with myself. I've had to take a wholehearted look in the mirror and search for truth in a quest for real freedom from the bondage that has held me back from shifting to my next level and shifting in God.

John 8:32 (KJV)- And ye shall know the truth, and the truth shall make you free.

This purge did not come about because I knew it was time to be bold and I was ready to look the things from which I needed purging straight in the face, but when you're not ready or don't know how, God will often push you to your next level, even without your knowing participation. You just have to be willing to let God into your heart, search you, and allow God to move however He sees fit.

Psalm 139:23 (KJV)- Search me, O God, and know my heart; Try me and know my anxious thoughts. (I love the way The Message Bible states this as well: "Investigate my life, O God find out everything about me; Cross-examine and test me, get a clear picture of what I'm about."

God knows what you're all about and who He's called you to be! He wants the very best for you!

Jeremiah 29:11 (NIV)- For I know the plans I have for you," declares the Lord, "plans to prosper you and not to harm you, plans to give you hope and a future.

The Praise

2 Timothy 1:7 (KJV)- For God hath not given us the spirit of fear; but of power, and of love, and of a sound mind.

The praise report is this: I don't have to be fearful of the things that I cannot change (i.e. the "payne" of my sister's passing nor the fear that comes from confronting those who violated me 25 years ago. It means that I've got the power to overcome molestation, abuse, heartache, and misery. The praise report is that I win and the gag is, I've always been a winner! Even when the enemy tried to impart treacherous, assignment-killing seeds that followed me from childhood into adulthood; of abandonment, guilt and shame which led to self-conscientiousness, low self-esteem and doubt. It means that love and a sound mind is what I *will* walk in with the strength to carry on during my personal season of self-identification.

Today, I encourage you to ask God to search your heart and show you your true identity and whether there is anything that has held you back from shifting to your next level. Maybe it's not major life-altering experiences like what I've encountered; maybe it's people in your life, situations of the past or distractions yet to come that can hinder you.

And if you have a strong sense of self-identity, keep growing as **Colossians 1:10** (NIV) states, so that you may live a life worthy of the Lord and please him in every way: bearing fruit in every good work, growing in the knowledge of God,". Our goal should continuously be to grow and shift to our next level.

Reference

The Holy Bible: Authorized King James Version. Nashville: Thomas Nelson, Inc., 2001. Print *New International Version, Women of Faith Study Bible.* Grand Rapids: Zondervan, 2002. Print *The Message Version.* Bible Gateway, www.biblegateway.com. Accessed 29 Jul. 2019. Web https://www.merriam-webster.com/dictionary/suppression

https://www.merriam-webster.com/dictionary/purge

CHAPTER THREE

KEEP HANGING ON, THE BREAKING IS FOR THE MAKING!

SHONQUIL JONES-DYSON

The Breaking

The enemy has a way of playing mind games that are sculpted to make you feel like you are losing your grip. Don't be tricked. Sometimes, we go through temporary tests that require more of our attention, but one thing I have come to know is, all will be well if you are anchored in Christ, so don't give up.

Two years ago, I found myself broken and depressed with two children, on a new path of independence. I was trying to endure a separation from my spouse and had no idea how I was going to juggle things. All I could see ahead of me was a struggle because I allowed the enemy to move in and plant fear. Even though divorce was not the case, my life was indeed changing fast. I didn't understand why I had been placed in a position that was intense and seemed too hard to bear. This unexpected change hit me during a time I felt most confident. It was in a season where things appeared to be working out for me. It is clear now that I was blinded from the truth because my focus was on goals I had set, not the plans God had for me. I had become too sure of my life within my terms. My blueprint was solid, and I was preparing to make moves to help my personal and professional life. Never once did I talk to God about it or involve Him.

Jeremiah 29:11 The Holy Bible NIV

For I know the plans I have for you, declares the Lord, plans to prosper you and not harm you, plans to give you hope and a future.

What I planned was not in line with the purpose God had for my life. I had many signs before a shift was sent, but I ignored them. When it manifested into bigger setbacks, the effect was strong enough to knock me to my knees. I lost sight of what mattered most; my salvation. While trying to set up a lifestyle I thought was best for me, I didn't realize I was placing myself outside God's will. Being outside His plan is the most dangerous place to ever end up. I believe God was my roadblock. To save my life, He shook it. God shut me down and abruptly put me in a place of correction. Yes, issues needed to be addressed in my marriage. Yes, I needed to change a few things and grow personally. Most importantly, I needed to trust God fully in all situations and just let go and let Him.

As far back as I can remember, I lived a life where I was sheltered from reality. Things just happened for me, and because I didn't know the level of sacrifice it took for those situations to work out, I easily took life for granted. I took my faith and blessings for granted. I was unintentionally running off conditional faith. I discounted the signs of my purpose because I did not think I was cut out to be the person God created me to be. How silly of us to tell God, who created us, who we are going to be. Most of us are guilty of this. Do not get me wrong, there is nothing wrong with wanting what's best for you and your family. However, it is not okay to lose yourself in the process. Sometimes, we get into the rhythm of our daily routines and without notice, we neglect our spiritual duties. My shakeup was sent to get my attention and to get me right back on track. At the time, I thought my life was over, and I could not bring myself to the thought of living the rest of my life, either single or with a new love. We had been together since teens. I thought if my marriage ended, it would be under the circumstance of infidelity or something as serious, I thought wrong. It was because of something seemingly light. The things that hit our relationship were workable, however, we both needed the tools and the time to work through them. God knew we loved each other, but we needed a season of enlightenment for the sake of personal growth. We could not be that special person the other one needed if we did not know who we were as individuals. One thing I have learned through the process is, you must be whole before trying to make it work as one healthy half of a relationship. How can you offer your half without another half to keep for yourself? You cannot survive off giving your complete source of energy to one particular entity and feel complete. There would be nothing left for you to grow from!

Isaiah 55:8-9 Holy Bible King James Version

"For my thoughts are not your thoughts, neither are your ways my ways, saith the Lord. For as the heavens are higher than earth, so are my ways higher than your ways, and my thoughts than your thoughts."

During this journey of new, challenging, and unwanted independence, I told myself that no matter what, I would survive, and succeed. The pressure I was feeling triggered early memories of the struggle I endured in silence. It was causing old habits to form again. During my early twenties after having my second child, I was diagnosed with clinical depression. I was embarrassed and confused as to how that could even be a part of me. I went to many doctors and therapists and took many medications. I was trying to erase this tag which was placed on me, and I wanted to hide. During that season of life, I told myself that if I ever made it to the other side of that emptiness, I would never fall that deep again. I did have a setback in 2013 after the unexpected death of my father, but I fought to stay off medication. Praying and listening to my doctors, I saw impressive progress. Appointments became fewer, and I was clear to live a healthy productive life. Taking a hit to my marriage at a time I saw myself healthy again after an eight-year battle was quite a charge. With so many things buried in my heart and even more struggles tormenting my mind, I was determined to fight. I was hurting, but I kept moving. Now living on my own with the kids, I successfully made all the necessary changes to my schedule, so I do not miss a major beat. I was able to get the kids to school, arrive to work on time and do the same for pickups. I had a plan for after-school practices and games. I could not just lay there and let life kick me while I was down. I had to pull myself together, activate my faith and allow God to work out details of my marriage. My spouse and I were going through a healing process; however, we had parenting down to a science. Eventually, I felt things were flowing well once again, and it became easy to breathe again.

I had a habit of learning to cope with my flaws instead of trying to fix them. Well, this time, that habit did not fly. I had to work on myself in order to move forward. Aside from planning daily routines, I was neglecting spiritual routines. I spent my Sundays in bed instead of in church. I made dinner dates and other plans take the place of Bible studies. It all happened unintentionally. One skip led to another, and I created one of the most detrimental patterns one could ever imagine, especially when going through life-altering trials. My prayer life died. While trying to stay above it all and let go, I turned away instead of holding on. I was not mad at God, but I was in a bitter place altogether. I lost the desire to pray, and that terrified me. I allowed situations weigh me down. Fighting in the physical left me little energy to fight spiritually. Each day I put it off to the next until it went too far. Know this, no matter how far you go it is never too far to repent and return in His loving arms.

Philippians 4:6-7 The Holy Bible KJV

Be careful for nothing; but in everything by prayer and supplication with thanksgiving let your request be made known unto God. And the peace of God, which passeth all understanding, shall keep your hearts and minds through Christ Jesus.

Before I came to terms with my mess, I had so much anger pinned inside, and it was manifesting into physical medical problems. My blood pressure was too high, my weight piled on, stress interrupted my sleep pattern, and I was always in a mood. It was strange because at the beginning of the entire situation, I was constantly praying and fasting, but as soon as things didn't turn out the way I had hoped, I gave up. There was my evidence of conditional faith. I had the nerve to be hurt because I thought God had turned His back on me, but that was not the case at all. I turned away from Him. God wanted me to realize how much strength I had. There were many times I would take the back end of a deal because I did not think that I was capable or worthy of leading. I discounted my knowledge and leadership skills because I did not think I looked the role; my self-esteem was so low. I learned how to play the part and never broadcast my insecurities. It only fuels those who lurk and wait for a chance to try and destroy you.

Though I was at my lowest point, I was determined not to stay there. God had placed some strong, wise women of God in my life, and they weren't going to let me fall either.

The Making

"You have everything you need to be the best you can be. You may be bent, but you are not broken. Know that all is well in the kingdom."
~Selene Anderson~

The best piece of encouragement I received was the reassurance that all was well in the kingdom. That holds so much power. The tears that flowed uncontrollably stopped after those words were spoken into my life. Within two years, God managed to do a work in me I never imagined was possible. The tears of hurt and disappointment were replaced with strength. Life has taught me education, money or social status does not make you exempted from trials. Faith taught me a dedication to the idea of succeeding no matter what makes the journey more hopeful. God does not place us in a situation without tools to get through it. He hears every prayer, and as any good father would, He supports his children. It took for me to get on the other side of depression to realize God is indeed a mind regulator. It was when I made it to the other side of a broken heart, that I realized God was a heart mender.

During the time I separated from my spouse, I learned that I was beyond the levels I gave myself credit for. I was indeed strong, smart and beautiful. I was capable of doing things on my own without the need for validation. For years I was a hindrance to my own growth. My marriage did not suffer only because of my insecurities, but it played a significant role. I lost myself in the role of wife, mom, daughter, sister, and friend. I was afraid to be in the front line because I did not like the person I saw in the mirror. I had issues rooted in my spirit from childhood losses, and I never healed from them. It manifested in my adult relationships. Everything that I went through prepared me for a time such as this. As a child, I always wanted to be in God's ministry and help people breakthrough from things that kept them bound. One thing I lacked was experience. How can I lead if I've never followed? How can I help the broken-hearted if I do not know hurt?

Hebrews 12:14 NIV

"Make every effort to live in peace with everyone and to be holy; without holiness no one will see the Lord."

Forgiveness was the road to our reconciliation. My spouse and I, through prayer and understanding, managed to find the love and friendship that was dying. We had to put aside the mentality of who is right or wrong and embrace the fact we were changing and that change was ok. Though we are joined together in marriage, we are individuals, with individual interests. We had to sit down and talk to each other, not at each other. Our determination to build strong communication skills kept us focused. I had to take time and learn the man my husband had become and he had to learn the woman I had become. After realizing the person, I fell in love with was still there and the love was still present, I was able to trust we were going to be ok. It certainly was not easy but I knew that the process was worth the outcome. Both individuals have to want it to work, the load is far too heavy for one. Today, we are indeed stronger than before. That shift was necessary and I'm so in love with this "new" love.

Corinthians 4:8-9 (NIV)

"We are hard pressed on every side, but not crushed; perplexed, but not in despair; persecuted, but not abandoned; struck down, but not destroyed."

Do not lose your blessing because you could not see the sunshine in the night. Trust the process. When life begins to seem unbearable, dig deeper and hold on tighter. I would not trade my journey for anything in the world. He saved me from me. I thought I was running things well, but I was wrong. I was on a slow fall to hell. The moment I let go and allowed God to have His way, He began to show me why I was created. He began to show me the love I thought I had lost. God is so amazing, and if you give Him a chance to prove it, it will change your life forever. Listen, if you have fallen and turned away, go back to Him. Allow Him to love you and lead. I promise you'll never regret it.

1Peter 5:10 (KJV)

"But the God of all grace, who hath called us unto his eternal glory by Christ Jesus, after that ye have suffered a while, make you perfect, stablish, strength, settle you. To him be glory and dominion for ever and ever. Amen."

CHAPTER FOUR

KNOW WHEN AND KNOW HOW

DR. CYNTHIA J. HINES

I Was Blind

I remember very clearly, over 20 years ago, someone gave me a piece of advice and I had no idea what it meant. A woman looked me straight in the eyes and said Cindy, "know when and know how" and she walked away. At the time I was very confused. I looked at her, scratched my head and said to myself, what is she talking about?

I worked at a chemical company and was attending a week-long facilitation training for management. It was years later, before I fully grasped what the female trainer was trying to tell me. I believe as one female to another she was trying to give me a clue.

In hindsight, I now realize I was likely overcompensating during class and it was obvious I was trying to fit in. I was the first black female leader in the company. I had good ideas, but I did not know when and how to effectively communicate those ideas. I was very outspoken, and I spoke my mind whenever I wanted. What I failed to realize was that when a person overcompensates it is not uncommon to hurt your own cause rather than help. My approach at times caused people to dismiss good ideas due to my presentation. This chapter, Know When and Know How, stresses the importance of spiritual maturity and self-awareness to lead a successful Godly life.

My story is a culmination of a lifetime of experiences, mistakes and missteps which led me to become spiritually mature and self-aware. Although I am much better, I am still learning more about myself as I continue to grow in Christ. During my life I always felt different and that I did not fit in. It took years of learning and the grace of God before I became comfortable in my own skin. For example, I found out the hard way that when people tell you, "just be yourself", there are unwritten rules. You cannot always fully expose yourself in unfamiliar surroundings. Be yourself is sometimes code for "be yourself as long as you";

- Don't make others uncomfortable.
- Don't shine too bright.
- Don't rock the boat.
- Don't upset the apple cart.
- Don't surpass others.
- Play by the rules.
- Go with the flow.
- Stay within certain boundaries.

And never forget you are still a woman living in a male dominated society. During my early career, I was totally oblivious to the unwritten rules. How am I supposed to know the unwritten rules, if no one bothered to write them down or tell me? I guess that is why they are called unwritten rules.

2
My Story

As the only black female supervisor at a chemical plant, I felt I had to stand my ground. Some of my male employees and colleagues were very supportive while others were not receptive to a black female boss. Some coworkers felt the need to constantly challenge me while others were glad to have me on the team. I worked for 20 years at the chemical company and managed to have a successful career. However, it was a very long and sometimes hard 20 years. At that time, I was in church, but I was not rooted in my faith. I had not mastered "when" and I was definitely on the struggle bus regarding "how".

I developed an unhealthy pattern of promotion followed by trying to prove myself. Typically, a person tries to prove them self to get the promotion; not me. I would get the promotion, then try to prove to others and myself that I deserved the promotion I had already received. Geesh, can you imagine my frustration? I had a broken mindset that comes from the lack of knowledge and spiritual immaturity. Looking back, I realize I was trying to fit in not knowing that God never designed me to fit in. God would not allow me to blend in even when I tried.

Like a heat seeking missile, people always found me out. They noticed there was something different. As it became apparent that I had a special talent, skill or ability; one of two things would always happen. Either someone felt threatened by my presence or I became overtaxed by trying to help everyone. Both paths can lead to self-destruction if you are not careful.

When others feel threatened it can put you in a defensive posture which in turn can lead you to react in unnatural ways. I never understood how someone I just met could dislike me. That was so odd to me. How do you know you do not like me if you do not even know me? But God revealed to me that we are children of light. It is the light in me that people respond to either positively or negatively. Darkness or children of darkness hate the light or children of light.

Therefore, when darkness encounters light it will immediately attack. Ephesians 6 New International Version (NIV)

12 For our struggle is not against flesh and blood, but against the rulers, against the authorities, against the powers of this dark world and against the spiritual forces of evil in the heavenly realms.

Like playing sports, you always want to play YOUR game. Never be forced to play someone else's game. Stick to the plan and be yourself. Do not react in response to others, it is a mistake.

Jesus never reacted to others. His mission was clear, and he stayed the course. Jesus was always about his Father's business and we as believers must do the same.

3

John 15:18-19 New International Version (NIV)

18 "If the world hates you, keep in mind that it hated me first. 19 If you belonged to the world, it would love you as its own. As it is, you do not belong to the world, but I have chosen you out of the world. That is why the world hates you.

When people positively respond to the light in your life, it can be a great feeling. However, the danger comes when people love you so much, they come to you for everything. You become the go to person at home, work, community and in the church. Stress and burn out is real. If you do not learn to say no to some good things, you will never get to those higher things that God has called you to do. Good things can be a distraction as well as bad.

In God's Design (Martens, 1998) said that "God's design is one which gives people a good measure of freedom, the path of progress toward the goal is not uniformly paced or even straight." I feel this quote describes my path well. 1 Although I had attained many achievements, the path to those goals have been anything but straight. When people lack spiritual maturity, they struggle daily at work, home, school, and in the community and church. They struggle because of the inability to discern what is really transpiring in the atmosphere.

I was a spiritual person many times in non-spiritual environments. I tried to survive with the use of my intelligence, political savvy and wit. At that time in my life, I lacked the knowledge and skill to use spiritual weapons such as peace, prayer and the word of God. As a matter of fact, I did not know how to identify when I was in a spiritual battle. That is why you must know when and know how. This approach is key in the natural and spiritual realm.

2 Corinthians 10:4 King James Version (KJV)

For the weapons of our warfare are not carnal, but mighty through God to the pulling down of strong holds;

Eventually I left the chemical company to pursue other opportunities. I began working for a hospital system and rose through the ranks of management to become the first black female at the director level among 80 leaders. When a person is "the first" in any category they often face challenges as a forerunner. The struggle is real, the attack of the enemy is real. The opposing dark forces working against you want to minimize your accomplishments. The enemy wants to make it seem as if you have accomplished very little. However, the forerunner lays the foundation for those that will follow. No building can stand without a solid foundation.

I now believe that efforts to prove yourself are a waste of time and energy. If I had not earned a seat at the table, the promotions would have never been given to me. It is easy for me to say these things today because I am no longer in those environments and God has healed my mind. Today I work as a leadership coach and consultant assisting others that are still in the trenches. In the corporate setting there is tremendous pressure to perform and produce outcomes.

Added to the pressure to perform, many work cultures are not conducive to kingdom

4

Principles. The combination of these conditions can make it near impossible for Christians to thrive in such environments. Fortunately, by my 2 nd career I was starting to learn how to fully integrate my work life and my spiritual life. The two should not be mutually exclusive. I had to learn for myself what the older saints already knew; you've got to take the Lord with you, everywhere you go.

At the hospital one of the employees on my team was a local minister. If I came into work in the morning and I said I had a headache, she would close the door and lay hands on me and began to pray. I thanked God for my personal prayer warrior at work. There were a few other women at work that were spiritual. The Lord allowed us to find each other, bond and to be supportive of one another. We remain connected to this day. I thank God my immediate superiors were men of faith. I found that while the workplace can be brutal at times; men and women of faith do exist there you just have to find each other. A Godly connection at work is extremely important for believers. Even in the bible the disciples were sent out in teams.

As the first woman on a national church ordination committee, I was concerned I would not be received well. I wondered how I would be received by the male elders. The committee had previously been men only from the churches' inception over 100 years ago. Fortunately for me I was well received by the other members of the committee. It was at that moment that I knew God was in the plan.

I have many other war stories but hopefully you get the picture. Spiritual maturity and self- awareness are critical to a godly life. Do not be deceived, more money, higher positions and more education does not mean you can get away with praying less because you have everything. This is a trick of the enemy that many believers fall victim to. If anything, I found the opposite to be true. The higher I ascended within organizations; I needed the Lord more not less. I encountered some malicious, manipulative and ungodly leaders that made me pray harder than ever before. Just remember when all hell is breaking loose around you, that God always has the final say.

The Story of Esther

One of my favorite bible stories is the story of Esther. Her uncle who raised her told her not to reveal her Jewish background to anyone in the palace. Esther was chosen from among many beautiful women to become the next queen. She would prove to be a deliverer of an entire nation. One of the most notable verses in the bible was spoken by Esther when she said;

Esther 4:16 King James Version (KJV)

Go, gather together all the Jews that are present in Shushan, and fast ye for me, and neither eat nor drink three days, night or day: I also and my maidens will fast likewise; and so will I go in unto the king, which is not according to the law: and if I perish, I perish.

5

Those famous words signify a woman that was willing to go the distance and risk everything for a higher purpose. She was a reluctant risk taker. She wanted to blend in, fade into the background, stay above the fray but God would not allow it. Her uncle Mordeci came to Esther and admonished her that her placement in the palace was far too important to wait and see what would happen to her people. As described earlier, eventually true believers will be called out. When you are called out and sometimes must standout just remember that greater is, He that is in you than he that is in the world. The Book of Esther reinforces the biblical truth that God is always in control. God wants us to forget about our struggles and focus on him.

Philippians 4:8 King James Version (KJV)

8 Finally, brethren, whatsoever things are true, whatsoever things are honest, whatsoever things are just, whatsoever things are pure, whatsoever things are lovely, whatsoever things are of good report; if there be any virtue, and if there be any praise, think on these things.

Winston Churchill said that "There comes a special moment in everyone's life, a moment for which that person was born. That special opportunity, when he seizes it, will fulfill his mission – a mission for which he is uniquely qualified. In that moment, he finds greatness. It is his finest hour." Winston Churchill's quote is very fitting and describes Esther's situation well. Her uncle, Mordecai, told her "who knoweth whether thou art come to the kingdom for such a time as this?" Just because she was the Queen, it did not mean that she would escape death.

Her uncle was right, and her obedience saved an entire nation.

If we worry about fitting in, more than walking in our calling, we affect others as well as our selves. Once Esther decided to request an audience with the king although she had not been called for as was the tradition. She was very precise in when and how she proceeded. Her every move was spirit led. She called for fasting and prayer, dressed the part, arranged a meal, prepared a table for the enemy and asked for HER life. She knew her husband adored her, and the people benefited from the king's love for his wife.

Now I See

For many years I was blind to the principles I described. But now I see that only the right action at the right time will bring about God ordained success. Do not miss out on your mission in life, God has a specific purpose for you. Discover your God given purpose, follow through and you will be blessed.

1 (Martens, 1998) God's Design: A Focus on Old Testament Theology

Chapter Five

The Blessing In My Brokenness

Gricelda R. Ramsey

August 9, 2018 was supposed to be the first day of the rest of my life. I know it sounds cliché', but it's the truth. I had finally made a life altering decision to take control over my life. And after five years, the day had finally arrived. However, I did not arrive at this decision and this day easily.

I guess by now you're wondering what happened on this day. Well, I had decided after struggling and going back and forth with myself, to have weight loss surgery. So August 9 was the date my surgery was scheduled to happen. I know some people may say she took the easy way out, and there was a point in this process that I felt the same way. I thought to myself, "I'm not so far gone that I cannot lose weight the natural way".

Meanwhile, my weight was steadily increasing. I also thought to myself, "Why would someone elect to have surgery when they are not sick". However, I realized that my weight had become my sickness. So, I educated myself on the process and the expectations. This day was the day I would get my release. You see, I felt like I had been trapped in this shell. I call it a shell because I knew who I was and how I felt on the inside.

I have had issues with my weight all my life. However, over the past 12 years I have felt trapped in an over 300 lb. frame. I had allowed my weight to become a prison. It became the prison that held my hopes, dreams, goals, plans and ultimately, my purpose…or at least that is what I had convinced myself. It had gotten to a point where I was self-sabotaging opportunities with doubt and insecurity about my weight.

I would talk myself out of going places and doing things especially if I had to walk or stand. I only engaged in activities and tasks that I had to do i.e. go to work, take my son to school, or pick him up from school, go to church, and engage in some activities for my son's school or for church, etc. My weight was hindering the things that I needed to do as a wife, mother, and my personal and professional needs. I would come home and just sit, watch tv, and play games on my phone because I started to lack motivation.

This became a major problem and a point of disappointment because I have always been a goal-oriented person, and a planner when it came to my life. However, a few years ago I became stagnant. I started to reflect over my life, and I realized that I had not obtained some of my goals. This brought me to a dark place emotionally. So, I decided that I needed to make some drastic changes in my life.

Now back to the first day of the rest of my life; today was my day. I had no fear, and I was so ready to make this shift. As I laid in the pre-op area, I was thanking God for this gift, the gift of getting a new start. I went in the operating room at about 10:50 am and my surgery was done before noon. Everything went well.

The next day, I could not go home because I could not keep fluids down, and I had severely painful gas in my body from the surgery; and I was very nauseous. I decided to take a nap because I was still on the morphine drip. While I was asleep, the nurse came in the room and abruptly woke me up to see if I was okay. I told her I felt fine, and she said we just got a call saying your heart rate is high. Naturally, I started to panic; I wasn't sure what was going on.

Suddenly, the doctor comes in with a few more nurses. They give me an EKG to confirm the diagnosis, and I'm hearing words like "V-tech", and "A-Fib". I looked over to my husband and said, "Baby, start praying". I knew at that moment I had to depend on the Lord. My heart rate was at 180, then 220, then, 230 and went as high as 295…they started giving me medication intravenously to bring my heart rate down. I was so scared, but the medical team reassured me that I would be okay. However, they were moving me to the surgical ICU unit to be monitored more closely and given medication through the IV.

During this time, my godmother arrived to see me and when I tell you, I had another prayer warrior on the battlefield. Yes Lord. She and my husband began to pray. The nurse on the unit was amazing. He continued to reassure me that I would be okay, but I'm watching every beat on that monitor. And praise God my heart rate started to come down and by 3:30 or 4:00 am, my heart was back to normal sinus rhythm. I was able to move back to a regular room after a day and a half, praise God. I was discharged the following day. So, in my mind I thought everything was fine, but then came the aftermath....

The Brokenness

When I got home, I was trying to adjust to my new normal. A new way to eat, moving differently, a new burst of energy, losing weight, and trying to embark on this new journey. Lo and behold, the bottom starts to fall out. Just like in Romans 7:21...I find then a law that when I would do good, evil is present with me. And within about ten days of being home, I'm back at the hospital because my heart rate starts to go up, and I think I'm in atrial fibrillation again.

I'm sitting in the emergency room frightened going through an EKG, blood work, and tests. I don't know what to think, I'm just calling on the name of Jesus to help me. My tests results are all normal. No A-Fib, no heart attack, regular sinus rhythm. They give me an injection to settle me. Diagnosis...**Anxiety**!

After a couple more emergency room visits, I realized that I've experienced medical trauma. The result of this medical trauma was anxiety. I am a therapist by profession, and I have treated multiple people who suffer from anxiety, but at this moment, I find myself in this lost place.

The anxiety started to progress, and I was in the emergency room multiple times thinking something was wrong with my heart. Back and forth to doctor's appointments for follow-up and dehydration. I had so many needle pokes, my arms were tired and bruised. Little by little, the anxiety took over my life.

I started to have trouble sleeping at night, difficulty being at home by myself, and difficulty driving alone. I was becoming dependent, and I was upset about it. I had to have people drive me and I could not ride on the freeway if there were no exits for long periods of time. I had to have someone sleep in my room with me at night when my husband was on the road in order to fall asleep, and I was barely getting any sleep because I would stay up late to avoid going to bed because that's when the anxiety would start, at bedtime.

I knew I was a child of God, but this was my reality. And no one could understand what I was facing. No one could understand that one of the best things to happen for me had become another form of imprisonment. I could not be happy about my weight loss and my new journey, and I started to have regrets.

I was in constant fear…fear of dying, fear of passing out and being home alone, just fear, fear, fear. I gained a whole new understanding about the power of fear. It was taking over. Thankfully, I was off work still. I realized that while I was in the hospital, I had around the clock monitoring, and I felt safe. I had no episodes of anxiety while in the hospital. However, when I came home reality set in. After a few days my husband had to go back to work (and he drove a truck and would not be home until the weekends); my sister who lives with me was at work, my son was away at school. So, I was alone with my thoughts and my fears.

The anxiety started to manifest in physical symptoms; rapid heart rate, ringing and full feeling in my ears, blurred vision, occipital nerve syndrome; tingling in my hands, arms and feet, and triggered my reflux; all of which I developed as a side effect of the surgery. As a result, I'm running to see this doctor and that doctor, to rule out this and rule out that. I have seen more doctors since this surgery then I can remember ever seeing.

The anxiety was becoming somewhat debilitating. I felt I could not go on like this…something had to give. I decided that I could not let this take over my life. I had to go back to work, I had to drive, I had lots of things going on in my life, and I did not want to become a prisoner to this problem.

Getting My Fight Back

First, I needed to figure out the ultimate source of this problem. As a clinician, I have had this conversation with many people with anxiety disorder, now it's like the doctor becomes the patient. This is different when you are the one going through it. Anxiety is based in fear and uncertainty. I had to understand that my fear was based in my medical trauma which made me have a perpetual fear in dying.

I started praying to God continually. The bible tells us to pray without ceasing, so I started running a marathon with prayer. After the fourth emergency room visit, I decided that I needed to get some help. The doctor was recommending medication to treat the symptoms. I was skeptical of taking medication, but I wanted this to stop. The medications have so many side effects and that made me more afraid. I tried a round of medication and it caused me to have multiple panic attacks in one day. So, I decided that I need to figure out a healthier way to manage my symptoms.

I started to go to yoga once per week, and I talked to one of my doctors who referred me to a therapist. I started coloring and I also had an app on my phone that was a color by numbers app. It has become the most relaxing tool in helping me to cope with anxiety symptoms. I started sharing my story and I called on my village; my support system. I started calling on my prayer warriors who were near and far to pray for me and with me. I knew how to plug into my source and my source was the Almighty God; and he was working through people.

One of the nurses in the emergency room even told me about a phone app that has meditation music and inspirational messages to help me to sleep at night, and it really did help me. I started reading and holding onto some scriptures to carry me through…2 Timothy 1:7 (King James Version), God has not given us the spirit of fear, but of power, and of love, and of a sound mind; Jeremiah 29:11 (King James Version), for I know the thoughts that I think toward you, saith the Lord, thoughts of peace, and not of evil, to give you an expected end;

Lamentations 3:22-23 (King James Version), the steadfast love of the Lord never ceases; his mercies never come to an end; they are new every morning; great is thy faithfulness. And my ultimate favorite was from Philippians 4: 6-7 (Amplified Bible), Do not be anxious *or* worried about anything, but in everything [every circumstance and situation] by prayer and petition with thanksgiving, continue to make your [specific] requests known to God. And the peace of God [that peace which reassures the heart, that peace] which transcends all understanding, [that peace which] stands guard over your hearts and your minds in Christ Jesus [is yours].

Ultimately, I had to decide to change my mindset. I began to rationalize my fears and face them. I started making myself drive alone, and I started to tell myself that if the Lord wanted to call me home, he would not necessarily wait until I fell asleep. I had to play over and over in my head and say out loud "I'm alright", "The doctors and tests all say that you are fine", and I was constantly rebuking Satan.

Day by day, I started to get better and stronger. Did I have setbacks or relapses, absolutely, especially when my sister died unexpectedly from congestive heart failure. I ended up in the hospital that same night. Do I still have periodic episodes of anxiety, absolutely? The difference is now I'm able to do self-talk, pray, breathe through it, and I recognize and understand the symptoms. And I go into fight mode and talk myself off the ledge. I'm getting my fight back.

The Blessing In My Brokenness

While this was by far one of the most uncomfortable and frightening experiences of my life, I was blessed with a platform to bring more awareness to mental health issues and the impact on people's daily living. When people think about mental illness or mental health, they envision someone who is psychotic or someone who is really unhinged and engaging in all sorts of behaviors. But anyone could be affected and through sharing my personal experience, I have encountered so many close family and friends, and people in the church who are experiencing some form of anxiety or other mental health issues.

Anxiety and atrial fibrillation have forced me to seize every opportunity, and I have been able to set some goals and start accomplishing them. I realized that life is short and fear and doubt are the biggest dream killers. I understand when you are at the end of your rope, but on the other side is your breakthrough.

The scripture promises that God remains with those who are broken and makes them stronger than before. He has given us three important promises in our brokenness; Deuteronomy 31:8, he will never leave you; 2 Corinthians 12:9-10, my grace is sufficient; and Romans 8:28, he works all things for the good. We should not run from being broken, even though it is uncomfortable or scary, because it will produce growth and a better life.

Brokenness is a blessing because it puts us on the road to a breakthrough. Jesus said, (in Matthew 5:3) "Blessed are the poor in spirit" for theirs is the kingdom of heaven. Those who are broken will be blessed because they will see God, and God's power will flow through their lives. Girl, I'm getting my fight back!

Reference:

(Philippians 4.6-7, *Amplified Bible Version*)

(Deuteronomy 31.8, 2 Corinthians 12.9-10, Romans 8:20, 2 Timothy 1.7, Lamentations 3. 22-23, Jeremiah 29.11, *King James Version*,)

Chapter Six

I Lost Some Battles But I Won the War

Monsenaray Sheppard

Who said you couldn't??? God said I can!!!!!

There was a time that I thought I could not achieve anything in life since everything I did amounted to NOTHING! In and out of jail and prison was the norm for me. I figured that I had to make my presence known each time I visited a place. If I happened to be in a club or part of a crowd, then everyone would notice me since I was the loudest. Everyone could realize my presence even at home because I thought that the personality of an individual was determined by how loud he or she was. That had been my character trait ever since I was a teenager.

Quitting school in 1975 at the age of 17, I found myself doing things grown folks did.

After all, I thought that my mindset was like that of an adult. I had no interest in school, and this was evident through the numerous times I was kicked out and had to repeat the 10th grade three times. I kept asking myself, how did I end up in such a situation? After thinking carefully about the things, I could be doing, my friends and I decided to drop out.

Life is a Journey: And so, life begins.

In 1976 at the age of 18, I found myself pregnant giving birth to a baby boy on February 14, 1977. By then, the movie Roots had been released and I decided to name my son after the actor. This would be the beginning for me in and out of jail trying to provide for the child. From 1981 to 1989, I went to prison five times not counting the times I spent in the county jail. Life was like a nightmare for many years. I was on a merry go round and I didn't know how I would stop it. I was not certain if I really wanted to change my behaviors, but I knew that there was more to life than what I was experiencing.

Where was the God I was taught about in Sunday school? If God loved me why was I going through all of this? Why couldn't I live a normal life if there was ever such a thing as a normal life? "I gave you to the Lord years ago". These were my mother's words echoing in my mind. "You are in God's hands, Monsenaray", she would tell me. I really did not know what she meant by those words. It wasn't until I reached the lowest point in my life that I came to realize what those words meant.

I made a vow to the Lord

During my fifth time in prison, and while walking around the yards, I began to talk to God in a way that I had never done before. Not to mention that I had made it a custom to talk to God and read the Bible whenever I got locked up. This particular time I was crying as I began to ask God why me? Lord why do you continue to allow me to spend my days, and even months, in and out of the prison system? These words came to my mind, **"Count it all Joy!"** I didn't understand what God was saying to me, but it kept ringing in my mind. **Count it all Joy!** When I got back into my room, I got my Bible and I found the scripture in James 1:2-3 "My brethren, count it all joy when ye fall into divers' temptations: knowing this, that the trying of your faith worketh patience". What are divers' temptations? In the Greek translation, Poikilois means many kinds, and Peirasmos means trials or difficulties. So, was God telling me to Count it all Joy whenever I fall into many trials? What was so joyous about the trials I had endured? How could joy come from the mess I had found myself in? My mother had told me that she gave me to the Lord many years ago. Everything was starting to make sense to me by then. God was allowing these things to happen to me, and I believed that it would later all work together for my good.

Romans 8:28 says, "And we know, that All things work together for the good of them that love God and who are the called according to his purpose". What I was going through had begun to make sense to me for the first time in my life. I realized that God had called me and there was a purpose for my presence in the world. I was taught to love Him as a young girl. David knew that if he fell in the hands of the Lord, he would be alright. David also knew that God was merciful and kind and would spare him in each circumstance. So, in other words, my mother knew that giving me to God would place me under His hands of protection. She knew that at God's timing I would surrender to his will and get my life right with God. So you see prison is not always bad. God had his hands on me all the time. Jeremiah 1:5 says "I knew you before I formed you in your mother's womb. Before you were born, I set you apart; I appointed you as a prophet to the nations".

In 1986, during one of the many times I had come home from prison, my mother told me that a prophetess from New York had asked her to stop crying and get up off her knees. She told her "Your daughter (Monsena) would be a Missionary since God is not yet done with her". At that time I told my mother out of sarcasm to inform the prophetess that I would not be anyone's Missionary. I did not know what I was saying, but God had his hands on me and I didn't realize it. Going back to prison two more times after that prophecy raised more doubt on the dream of becoming a missionary.

There is victory on the other side!

It was good for me that I had been afflicted!!! It was good for me! Yes, this was David's prayer in Psalms 119:65-72, "Thou hast dealt well with thy servant, O Lord, according to unto thy word. Teach me good judgment and knowledge: for I have believed thy commandments". He went on to say in verse 67, "before I was afflicted, I went astray: but now have I kept thy word". Then down in verse 71, David says "it was good for me that I have been afflicted; that I might learn thou statues". In other words, David was asking God to teach him good judgment. I realized that it was good for me to go through hardships so that God would make me understand my purpose in life.

For the last time in 1989, I was released from the women's prison in Ypsilanti, Michigan. With a made up-mind and the Lord's help, I promised myself that I would do what was expected of me and that was to serve the Lord. By then I was in my 30's, and without hesitation, I began to attend church just I did when I was a little girl. God met me at my point of brokenness and began to work on my heart and mind. I remember my Bishop saying to the church one Sunday that those who wanted to be delivered from anything had come back to the church that Sunday night, and I thought to myself this would be my night. On that Sunday night, I found myself at church, I was expecting something from the Lord for the first time. It was the night of my life-changing experience with God. Since that night, my life has not been the same. It is after that deliverance that I began to say "YES" to the Lord. I didn't understand what I was saying, but all I knew was that I wanted more of God and less of the world. We never know where our "YES" will take us, but God does!!!!

In 1995, one of my aunts in Lawton, Oklahoma needed assistance with some house chores because she and her husband had retired from the Military. She was also bedridden and had been in that situation for several years. By then, it was the sixth year since I was released from prison, and I was actively involved in church activities serving the Lord with my whole heart, mind, and soul. I thought that moving to Oklahoma to care of her was all I was going to do, but little did I know that God through His infinite wisdom had a different plan for me. My aunt passed on one year after I had moved to Lawton, Oklahoma, and since then, it became my training ground. I became a part of a small church with approximately 30 faithful members: God used me in that church. After serving the church for 6 months, my pastor appointed me to be the Missionary President a position that I held for three years. Of course, the prophecy that was spoken about me to my mother that I would be a Missionary one day came to my mind. Not only was I a Missionary, but I was also appointed the Missionary President. I had never held the position of a Missionary President before and, hence, God was preparing me for leadership. It was during that period that I accepted my call to the ministry, and I was licensed in 1998. For 18 years, I stayed under that leadership supporting and doing what was asked of me, and I can surely attest to being blessed by the Lord. The church grew and God was magnified. I did not always agree with everything, but I stayed there steadfast in doing the work of the Lord. Not only was I the president of the Missionary Department in my local church, but I went on to become the Director of my local church Missionary Department as well as the Chaplain of the Missionary Department in the State of Oklahoma. I also became the 2nd Vice President of the State of Oklahoma Missionary Department. We don't know where our "Yes" will take us, but just know that God promised to never forsake us. All He wants is a "Yes" and He will do the rest.

I have to get my fight back;

I will start by going back to school and finishing where I left off in 1976

Education and Sanctification makes a good combination, so I decided to go back to school. In 2004, when I was 44 years old, I went back to school for a nursing degree. With a G.E.D., I applied for a 4-

year college program and I was accepted. Things that I had never dreamt were now becoming a reality, and it was during this time that I confirmed that God knows the thoughts and the plans that He has for us. The thoughts of good, and not of evil, were now evident in my life. As I began to study for my degree program, I started facing some challenges. I began to go through some marital problems which is something that I thought would never happen. My husband and I were happily married and both of us were in ministry at a wonderful church. However, after 12 years of marriage, we allowed the enemy to come in. So, I found myself in the same situation as the one I was facing before. Hence, it seemed as if I was losing the fight. With much prayer, I decided to walk away and trust God. By now I was convinced that the Lord would see me through as He had always done. Unfortunately, the marital problems resulted in a divorce. It was after the divorce that I decided to take a C.N.A. class to get certified, and it seemed to be a good plan because the idea of becoming a nurse seemed so far-fetched. After getting my certification, I was immediately hired by one of the hospitals in Lawton, Oklahoma. Apparently, age was catching up with my parents which implied that they needed assistance. Maybe God had prepared me for such a time as this to care for my parents. After much prayer, I decided to move back to Michigan and assist my parents. After moving back to Michigan, I applied to the University of Michigan-Flint. All the credits from my previous college were accepted, and I immediately started my classes. Competition and time were against me since age was quickly catching up. After all, most of the students who had enrolled in the nursing program were young girls who had just left high school. I found myself in my 50's still trying to get my degree but giving up was not an option. I had lost too many times before, but I decided that I would not give up. After talking to one of my professors, I decided to change my major to Bachelor of Arts Degree majoring in Health Care Administration.

All things will work together for our good if only we will trust the process and the journey. The Fight is on!

Never allow anyone to tell you that you **Can't** because God said we can do all things through Him who strengthens us. When we were children, our parents would tell us that the word **Can't** is not in the dictionary; hence, it never existed in my mind. **God said I can!** I will tell you that through all my life's experiences, God has proven Himself in my life. So far, God has really blessed me, and in April 2018, I graduated with my Bachelor of Arts degree from the University of Michigan at the age of 60. I am now working on a Master's of Divinity (Religious Studies). It is only through God's help that I managed to make that achievement. Immediately after graduating, I got a job offer for an Administrative Assistant to the Chaplain at the biggest hospital in Georgia which is in Atlanta, and this is currently where I work as a C.N.A. Also, let me mention that I got an email for a job offer as well with the Clinical Recruiter Talent Acquisition Team in Human Resources at the same hospital. God is so merciful and kind and He cares about us. Many days I walked prison yard not knowing where my life was headed and I didn't realize God's plan in my life. All the time God had his hands on me. He knew I would be where I am today because He is an all-knowing God. I am back in the fight and it's already fixed. **I WIN!!!!!! Because God said I can! I GOT MY FIGHT BACK!**

CHAPTER SEVEN

"UNDISPUTED"

KIBRA VANHORN

Round One: Prodigal Daughter

I thought it was all good. I had given my life back to Jesus, in April of 2010, after being out in the world for over 10 years. Two warnings the preacher issued that day stuck with me: 1. Give your life to Christ today, because tomorrow may not come and 2. As soon as you make a decision for Christ, the devil will be plotting against you. I was 32 then, a single mother of two boys aged 13 and six at the time.

So, I went all in on my new Christian journey. You see, I was raised Seventh Day Adventist and had moral and ethical values instilled in me that I was determined to get back to. I joined the choir, became a church clerk, a deaconess (the youngest) and I helped in any area where help was needed. I kept the Sabbath, from sunset Friday evening to sunset Saturday evening. I even got married (although my mother begged me not to marry him). I was no longer living in sin, right? I was following the rules. And life was all good! That is, until I was diagnosed with Multiple Sclerosis (MS) six months after my wedding. That's when all hell broke loose.

Round Two: Trial By Fire

The symptoms started the day after the wedding. John was not thrilled to be obligated to someone who was having all these health issues. While I was sick, he was mean, petty and even had the nerve to cheat on me with (I found out later) several women. The doctor had told us that "MS patients in the US do experience a decrease in life expectancy."(Boston University, 2014) So, basically, he said, I would die younger. Hubby was not mentally or emotionally ready for the "through sickness' part of the marriage. Months later, I fell extremely ill and was hospitalized for the first time. The symptoms were overwhelming: extreme dizziness, head pain, muscle tremors, paralysis in my legs, numbness and tingling (in my face, arms, legs and vaginal area) partial blindness in my right eye, confusion, memory loss, muscle weakness and most of all, *extreme* fatigue. While my body started a riot, I started having a pity party.

I lay in that hospital feeling extremely sorry for myself. I wondered, "Why was God allowing this to happen to me?" My memories went to being raped as a teenager, then my life's downward spiral, and the plunge into alcoholism and promiscuity. I was emotionally and sexually confused. I had become a walking statistic. My life was in turmoil, but God sent Angels to rescue me in the form of three saints from my church. They kept ministering to me. Through their kindness, the Holy Spirit coaxed me back into Jesus' loving arms.

Now, I was doing everything I could to stay on the straight and narrow path. So, *WHY* was this happening now? What did I do? Slowly sadness and grief gave way to discernment. I knew God loved me! Didn't He protect me while I was OUT THERE? Yes! Plus, He promised not to leave me comfortless. I had faith in MY God. Through my tears, I opened a Bible (which seemed to magically appear on the bedside table). I turned to a chapter I had never seen before (read James 5:13-15). That was it! I was deeply encouraged by this and saw it as a sign from God. I praised God right then, because I knew my healing was coming!

While experiencing this major MS flare I had my first chance to be a witness for Christ during this battle. That same day, my very best friend came to the hospital to see me. She started crying after learning the prognosis and that there was no cure for MS. I hated seeing her so sad. I quickly told her not to worry because I would be fine. I assured her that Jesus went through worse than this. If He could get through that, then, surely, I could deal with MS. But she didn't understand what I meant.

I proceeded to tell her how Jesus died for our sins and what He had to go through during His journey to the cross. She still didn't quite understand what that had to do with me. I ended up telling her the whole redemption story. I started with creation, Adam and Eve and the plan that God and His Son came up with to save us from ourselves. She was truly amazed! It was then that I understood that I needed to go through *this* in order to help someone else *out*; to be a witness of Jesus Christ. Over a year later, my friend was baptized! In some way, that was the beginning of my healing. I got out of the hospital and things slowly got better.

Round Three: Fight

MS was not done messing with my life. I had to drop out of college because I was having trouble concentrating. I was getting frustrated because my A's started turning into C's and D's. My hands were weak and trembled all the time. I couldn't hold a pen or pencil right. I couldn't remember or recall common words and forgot simple things quickly. My pride was hurt because I had always excelled academically, especially when it came to English and grammar. Being a writer and a poet as well, made these issues particularly frustrating. And I was extremely tired all the time!

My job as a teller, at a well-known bank, also was affected. I was sick a lot, so it was frustrating for management, my co-workers, and emotionally, for me. Sometimes people treat you bad when they don't understand or lack empathy. And my doctor advised me to lose weight because being over or under a normal weight was not good for an MS patient. I definitely wasn't looking or feeling my best after being on steroids for months. I was 234 lbs at 5'2.

One day I decided that I'd had enough! Enough…of pain, frustration, fear and sadness. I wanted my life back! I filed for divorce from my cheating husband, joined a gym and started exercising. I also started writing again. I prayed about everything. I asked God to help me get through the divorce, help me lose weight, to humble me and help me find a new job. He started answering my prayers, first through Spoken Word Poetry. While participating in this art, I began to be fulfilled, spiritually, by letting my words tell my story and helping me to grieve and heal. I started feeling better physically and emotionally.

Round Four: Miracle On St. Thomas Street

In late January 2014, I began experiencing another MS flare. I went to work anyway because of the previous mental backlash from the workplace. I looked a hot mess. Extremely fatigued, I know I had to be moving in slow motion. My doctor had me walking with a cane. I had just turned 36. In February, a customer, who happens to be a pastor, came to my teller window. He immediately asked me what was wrong with me. I told him about the MS. He demanded my phone number and I felt compelled to give it to him. He said he needed to speak to me about this disease of MS. When he called I was busy. When I finally remembered to call back, I thought about texting because it was late, but I felt compelled to call anyway.

It was during that phone call that I was healed of the demon we call Multiple Sclerosis. He helped me understand that it was faith in Jesus that healed the sick in the olden days. He asked me did I have faith. And I did! He said a prayer over me repeatedly. Suddenly, I began to feel full… of God, His love for me and I felt like He was wrapping His Arms around me! Never have I experienced that much clarity of mind, peace, understanding, joy, love and Faith (all at the same time!) in my Savior! It was something I wouldn't believe happened unless it happened to me.

It was beautiful, but ugly as well, as my body purged itself through my nostrils (I won't describe it here). I started jumping up and down and shouting like the people I saw at church on TV! I could walk without a cane. My vision was perfect. The dizziness, tingling and numbness; all gone! I had NO MORE PAIN in my head! My mind was crystal clear and I felt energetic!

The pastor warned me not to allow this demon to return in my life or it would be worse. He said to fill my mind with things of God and to stay away from negative people and influences and keep my head in the Word. To say I had been healed is an understatement! I felt Brand New! My nightmare had ended!

Round Five: Like A Dog Returns to Its Vomit (Prov 26:11)

Lust is like a pet monster; if you feed it and play with it, it will grow into a Demogorgan. I hadn't had even one MS sign or symptom for 16 months after my healing. So if you're reading this, just know that I thought I was jammin. Seven months post healing, I started seeing an old flame named Alvin. But Alvin didn't believe in God! And I knew this. Don't ask me why, but I thought I could change his dark, bitter mind. (Note to self: stop trying to play God!) The abusive talk and body shame he began hurling at me was, ironically, what pushed me to seek a personal trainer. I had already lost 30lbs on my own and

Alvin's insults caused me to get really serious about my physical fitness. His abuse was a catalyst. But I didn't realize his bad spirit was infecting me. I didn't understand how I was slowly poisoning my body and spirit.

To this day I claim to be a dominant person. But there are some who can either force you or gently bend you to submit to them. Daemon was one of them. He was the person I chose to help me get fit. He, also, was someone I had vowed to stay away from because of the hold I felt he had on me when we dated in 08'. It felt too.... *carnal.* I now know it was my spirit that had me avoiding him afterward. I don't know why I proceeded *THIS* time (which further shows me that my decision-making sucked!)

I guess I saw the results he was helping others achieve and had temporary amnesia because of what I wanted. He eventually talked me into sleeping with him and it was a done deal after that. I look back now, and realize I did not have enough wisdom to deal with someone with such manipulation skills. Especially with me having as much brain damage as I did. But I thought I knew what I was doing. Soon, my life became all about him and only him.

Three months after dealing with Daemon, I slowly began to fall apart. I wasn't going to church as much. I felt guilty and ashamed of what we were doing. Oh, I didn't tell you he was also still dealing with his baby's mother. Never mind all the excuses and promises of leaving her; I *KNEW* better. She also knew about me. I was a glorified side chick. And I just couldn't pull myself away from him. He was very demanding and controlling. He would go into rages, and had extreme highs and lows. I tried to be perfect for him because I was afraid of not being perfect for him. I began to experience extreme anxiety when I thought he might become upset with me. So, I started praying, begging God to get him out of my life. Eight months in I was emotionally stressed and began having MS flares back to back, causing even more brain damage. In the midst of the sickness, Daemon got married. I was shocked yet relieved, but I knew God was answering my prayers! He was severing the unholy soul tie formed between us.

Round 6: Setup to Comeback

In my severance package God sent healing once more. He sent friendship and also a partnership in business. Because I had been groomed as a trainer, I decided to continue that route. A friend and I opened a fitness center together and became certified personal trainers. I received treatment for the MS and have not experienced a flare up since November 2015! God also sent me Real love. I fell in love with Nate, a wonderful, eye opening and spiritually conscious man, who has embraced me for my flaws and all. He is a beautiful spirit that encourages me.

God continues to open doors and present opportunities, which are fulfilling to me. I have discovered a passion for people through utilizing my spiritual gifts of Exhortation, Faith and Discernment. I love to motivate people through health & fitness. I have been an actress in a stage play and now have a weekly radio show. With this amount of brain damage, I'm not supposed to be able to do any of this. I still have many issues that I get through on a day to day basis but I choose to live a positive life on purpose. When I'm weak, my strength comes from the Lord.

Round 7: True Transformation

In February 2014, I heard a sermon I'll never forget. The preacher said that God allows some things to happen to us in order to perfect our character, so that we can make the shift to Heaven. At the time, it really moved me because it helped me understand that God wasn't punishing me. He was re-shaping me. I now understand that I was being humbled, to become submissive to Him but aggressive in doing the work He has for me. EVERYTHING, good or bad, helped push me to the next phase in my life. You see, God needed me to understand what others are going through or have been through to develop a deeper love for people. I had to become selfless.

I have survived sexual assault, church hurt, alcoholism, heartbreak, pain, an incurable disease, depression, foolishness and my own pride, among other things. I had to fight for my life but the old Kibra had to die. I'm not perfect but the Jesus In me, the One Who really fights For me, IS! And I'm no longer a walking statistic. I'm simply, God's child. During the trials (and there will always be trials) Jesus will never leave me alone or let me Stay down. He's doing everything He can to keep me close to Him. Thank You, Lord! I have committed my life to God and refuse to lose Heaven after going through so much hell. And I will continue to have faith no matter what the devil tries to hit me with especially, since Jesus has already won this thing with a TKO.

For Alma, Jeffery, Richie, Ron Small, James Lee & Sally Carr

References

Boston University Medical Center. (2014, January 21). Study finds decreased life expectancy for MS patients. ScienceDaily. Retrieved July 30, 2019 from www.sciencedaily.com/releases/2014/01/140121104245.htm

Chapter Eight

It's a Faith Fight.....Fighting to the Finish

Cassonya Carter

Have you ever been in a place where God has delivered you and carried you through some of the worst storms of your life, only to find yourself fighting another round of this thing called life? I have. Just when I thought I was done and able to breathe a sigh of relief, I get knocked down on my knees again.

I'm happy but I desire to be happier. I'm healthy but I desire to be healthier. I love me but there are still some things about me that I'm not in love with. I have a close relationship with Christ but I desire to be closer to Him. I am satisfied in my singleness but I desire to have that special someone God designed just for me in this season of my life.

I'm satisfied with my career but I know there is more that I need to do to make an impact. The fight is real but this time it is more internal.

External factors are contributors that influence the attack for each battle. Sometimes those things that caused you to fight in the first place return to you in a whole new way and completely catch you off-guard.

When God gave me the Seven Ds of my life — Disease, Death, Divorce, Depression, Deliverance, Discovery and Destiny — to get to "My Genesis," I thought it would be smooth sailing because I was finally conquering what I was afraid to confront. I was holding steadfast to that triumph. I overlooked the fact that because God had set me free and I was walking into the destiny of my purpose did not mean I would be free of trials, test and tribulations. I was under the impression that if I faced those things that had me bound, I would be free. I was literally holding on to the words in John 8:38: "He whom the Son sets free is free indeed." I was free but had not maintained my freedom. The unexpected blows of the fight/situation caused my faith to waver. I was so busy focusing on the problem, I lost sight of the promise.

The Seven Ds of my life continued to manifest, but this time in a different manner, forcing me to rely on God much more than ever. The statement "I fought a good fight" resonated within my spirit. I'm starting to see how some of those old sayings and songs have new meaning in my life today. Such as "You will understand it better by and by," "Lord help me to hold out," "I need Thee, Oh I need Thee," to one of one of my all-time favorites "Faith that can conquer ANYTHING."

You see, I am the type of person who tries to handle things all by myself. This way, I don't have to be disappointed. If things don't turn out or come to fruition, I only can blame myself or hold me accountable. After all, you can only change yourself, right? Little did I know that this method of coping was triggering more harm than good, causing a battle inside my mind. I found myself battling anxiety, self-acceptance and at times self-confidence. Anxiety happens when people feel that they have to figure out everything all by themselves. They worry about even the simplest things because they are uncertain about the outcome. They panic or stress when things go wrong or think of what may happen. How could I let this happen to me, where was my faith? Why wasn't my faith in God as strong as I thought it was? Then it hit me, I was in a "Faith Fight." This was not a trick of the enemy but God teaching me how to have total faith in Him.

Doctors found a better treatment that kept my ulcerative colitis and Crohn's disease under control with a drug that has limited side effects. My hair was starting to grow back, but I was still a little disturbed that it was thinner than my normal. I had to get the big chop. I was struggling because I only knew how to work with my hair long. While I realize, I am not my hair, nor does it define me, but the condition that I was fighting was a reminder of my past and how this disease changed my life. If another person asked me why I cut my hair or said to me, "It is just hair," I was going to scream!

God had me right where He wanted me. I witnessed the journey of an 8- year-old girl who I knew battled a rare form of cancer. She did it with so much faith, poise and gracefulness. I watched her decide to have all her beautiful long cut off before the effects chemotherapy and radiation would make it fall out. She smiled through it all and even had a henna design placed on her head. I was convicted and had to repent in this faith fight. I asked the Lord to please forgive me for feeling sorry for myself. There are so many people battling diseases that have made them lose all their hair and I'm fretting because my disease thinned mine, made it shed so much and it needed to be cut. This faith fight was a humbling round. I'm happy to announce that that little girl had the chance to ring the bell as a sign of the end of her chemotherapy. God allowed me to learn so much from her.

Trips to hospital emergency rooms have decreased and my hospital stays have been minimal to none. Even with this positive regimen, my hormones were changing due to menopause. This combined with the new medicine and menopause was causing a case of acne. I never really struggled with acne before. An occasional breakout here and there while growing up during my cycles but the pimples never hurt underneath like this, nor were they so big that they left marks on my face for days. I was flustered to the point that I was so self-conscious.

In addition, my menopause was slowing down my metabolism, which made working out seem like a waste of time. I had manage to keep most of the weight I lost after my last hospital stay off. Rather than celebrate what I kept off, I stressed about what I gained back. I shared my struggle with my health coach. The coach reiterated that with auto-immune diseases, I will encounter various shifts with my body as well as my emotions, I must not quit striving to maintain a healthy lifestyle. I was reminded of a post from my Soulful Motion coach on our Facebook page that had my picture with the message, "When you feel like quitting, remember why you started." I stared at the picture long and hard as tears began to fall. In the picture I had a Soulful Motion "Jesus over Everything" shirt on, and I recognized that God was using this to elevate my faith. It encouraged my faith to persevere and continue to fight.

The angel of loss resurfaced in my life again. The man who had become my surrogate father passed away. Someone who looked after me when my own father passed, gave me wise counsel, gave it to me straight like I needed to hear it and always loved me like his own daughter. In addition, my Bishop made an announcement that he was stepping down as our Pastor to take an assignment from God in another state. Even though this was not a physical death, I was combatting another loss in my life.

While I was thankful that my surrogate father was no longer suffering, happy that my Bishop had an opportunity be nurtured and grow in the ministry, the dynamics of this shift were devastating. I did not think this would affect me like it did. Here I was facing yet another change in my spiritual and personal life, which brought another level of anxiety or anxiousness. I was growing in my relationship with Christ and my one-on-one walk with God but I still felt the pain of the loss — another faith fight.

We live in a time where the world is dealing with so many mental health issues, and recognizing the signs of depression are discussed in the media almost daily. Depression is real. We as Christians tend to think we are not vulnerable to this but in reality we are. When you are trying to do the right thing, be the right/best person, live the right way or just be a good/honest Godly person, the pressure in itself can be stressful. I found myself wearing another "mask." You walk around like everything is OK when deep down inside it is not.

I love the words of affirmation from one of my choir daughters, who is now a renowned motivational speaker — Shannon Cohen author of "Tough Skin Soft Heart." She shares the inner thoughts of her mind through her pen to empower people, especially women. Recently, I saw a phrase she created, "No More: Fake "I'm Fine." It spoke to me so deeply because I good at saying I'm fine when I'm really not. The day I saw that phase, I realized I had been wearing the fake "I'm Fine" mask. One of my favorite phases of hers: "Just because you are going through the fire does not mean you have to smell like smoke." What this phrase has taught me is that I can take off the mask, I no longer have to "fake it till I make it." All I have to do is "FAITH it till I make it."

In this faith-fight cycle, I was allowing anxiety of the shifts of life permission to hold me hostage in my thoughts. God sent a message through a conversation with one of my Sorority sister, and message on two different prayer calls about being anxious for nothing but in everything with prayer. I am thankful to God I recognize the signs, know how to seek help and don't have a problem with going to counseling. I have found an excellent faith based practice. Through my counseling sessions, I've learned the difference between situational types of depression — life changes that cause anxiety but you pull yourself together and move on — and clinical depression, which is a mental health disorder that can make you consider self- harm to yourself or someone else.

Regardless of the type of depression, situational or clinical, prayer, faith and professional counseling can be a winning combination in this round of a faith fight. You must be willing to face your "opponent" in order to defeat the attack or surround yourself around people that have your back. We all will encounter an experience of some type of depression in our lifetime; even the strongest Christian will encounter a season of unhappiness or dismay. Thank God for Isiah 41vs 10 (NIV) to coach us through the battle. *"So do not fear, for I am with you; do not be dismayed, for I am your God. I will strengthen you and help you; I will uphold you with my righteous right hand."*

I have entered the ring again and have crossed the threshold of the season of dating. I looked in the mirror one day and said to myself, "Girl, you've been married, divorced, single now what?" The level of anxiety that comes with the "now what" is mind blowing. I've been on several dates, some more consistent than others. I have met some interesting people. The agony of the being alone, possibility of being hurt, disappointed or even just not compatible with someone clouds my head on occasions wondering my outcome.

I have gone on dates with some really nice guys. They were really good people. When you want the more of God, good is not always acceptable. I want more than just a good thing; I want a God thing. Adopting this type of mentality means that I have to rely TOTALLY on God. Whenever, I felt I was "feeling some kind of way" about someone, I have this question I would petition God in order assure it was OK to open my heart more. I would simply say, "Lord, friends or more, I want what you have in store." When it does not work out the way I want it, yes, I may be disappointed and at times, have an attitude with God. However, when all is said and done, I realize God was working it out for my good.

Although I gained a few good friends, delayed does not mean denied. God's "no" is not saying that the nice man was not a good catch. All He was saying is that may be the one you want but he is not the one I have designed for you to experience the unconditional love I have required for you. I thank God that in this round of my faith fight, I have implemented the mindset not to settle in my singleness. More importantly, God has given me the peace of being alone but not lonely.

What I am learning is that God is keeping me in perfect peace while He is molding and maturing me, He is sculpting the piece that He has to complete my puzzle. God keeps providing me with what I need to show myself that the one He has designed for me will love God so much that he will fight for me, work with me and together as a team to make it to the next round in our faith fight. Until this happens I will increase my faith and fight till my change comes.

The Bible says in Mark 11:23, **"Whosoever shall say to the mountains in our lives to move out of our way and cast them into the sea; and shall not doubt in his heart, but shall believe that those things which He says shall come to pass; you shall have whatever God says."** I recognize that just because God said I could have what I say, it does not mean it would come easy. In order for me to appreciate what God has allowed me to have, I must work for it. It must be cultivated. The blow can knock you to your knees. Functioning on a "win" and not preparing for the next fight.

My minister of music asked a profound question one Sunday morning as we were preparing to minister through song. He said, "How do I find peace when I am missing a piece." The revelation was serial.

I've been floating on broken pieces. In order to continue to be what God has called me to be, new levels mean I will have to encounter new devils/obstacles. The Bible tells us not to be weary in well doing for in due season we shall reap if we faint not. Even though Galatians 6:9 is encouraging, I still get tired of fighting even though I know there is fight left in me. I've been taught to hold my peace and let the Lord fight my battles, victory shall be mine. I've learned and experienced that there are times when God will test your faith to see if you trust Him enough to fight for Him and building His kingdom. Trusting God when the blows hurt and are gut wrenching. When fighting these types of battles, you may feel very vulnerable, but this is not a bad thing, it builds your faith. Not all faith fights are an attack of the enemy. There are times when God wants to get the best out of us so He sends a little pressure.

I can't go backwards, I must press forward, and call things as they are and look at things as they were. I must press towards the mark of the high calling in Christ Jesus. I can no longer allow the enemy or the enemy inside of me hold me hostage in my yesterday. I must remember that yesterday prepared me for today to plan for my future to walk in my purpose. I must not allow those things that were not so favorable in my life to keep me from moving forward especially in my thought process and in the corners of my mind. I must hold tight to the promises of God and not get stuck in discouragement. They say that is easy to praise God when everything is OK. But they never talked about what happens when everything is OK and you're still battling the things that had you bound. The attack was similar in character just elevated to another form. There is reassurance in this faith fight knowing that the weapon formed but it won't prosper.

When you are in a faith fight, you must be committed confronting each round head-on. There are various types of rounds that will startle you, sting a little, throw you off balance and catch you totally off-guard. Then there are those rounds that will knock you right off your feet and, at times, leave you flat on your face. Trials are not our final destination, it's a method of transportation that takes us in the direction where we need to go. The challenge before us is: will we follow our own instructions or God's?

Just because the fight is fixed and you know that with God you can conquer anything, I'm learning you still have to fight, it's a part of the process. Even in the process you grow weary, you get disappointed and frustrated but you can't lose focus. You must continue to pray asking God to lead you all the way. You must trust God no matter what. We won't always see what God is up to, we just must remind ourselves He is up to something. Now, I understand that statement I heard about trusting God even when you can't trace him. I have to hold on to the promise that God is working things out for the good. Sometimes our faith is tested so that God can prune us, mold us, shape us and make us into who He's called us to be.

I find myself constantly saying though He slay me, Lord I will continue to trust You. I remember having a conversation with my brother about a lot of things that I changed because I wanted more of God. I remember telling him how the standards I set in this season of my life, weren't favorable or popular. I recall my brother saying to me, "You got to put a demand on God, He said He will give us the desires of our heart." In this faith fight, I must remember Hebrews 11:6 (KJV) "But *without faith it is impossible to please Him: for He that cometh to God must believe that He is, and that He is a rewarder of them that diligently seek Him*".

Sometimes we feel that when the storm is over we are home free because the sun is shining again in our life. But we forgot that even in the sun we can get burned. That is why we need God's rain to reign in our lives to grow and blossom. Sure, we can and will always get our fight back but we must continue to prepare ourselves for the next round or match or life circumstances. We prepare by growing closer to God, we prepare by reading His word, we prepare by strengthening our faith walk by putting on the armor because another fight will come, and the question we must ask ourselves is are we prepared for this fight? I know that it will come but I started telling myself it may knock me down but I refuse to let it knock me out.

My life is worth the fight, my life is changing. I am learning so much about myself in the midst of each battle and faith fight. Understanding God is my only hope. He is in my corner, in my ear like the manager of a boxer. God is in my ear instructing me how to prepare for the next round. All I have to do is follow His instructions. I may be bruised and battered but each time I go back to my corner of the ring, God nurtures every wound, every hurt, every cut, every bruise and every place that is swollen from some of life's direct hits.

We must always remember that our faith needs a picture of where we are going, faith has no limits, faith has no boundaries, faith in God has divine timing and we must elevate our faith to the level of the famine that we are fighting. I can't change what comes my way or what fight I may encounter but I can change my perspective on it and how I equip myself for the battle. My faith must be stronger than the battle itself. What is in front of me is not as strong as the power behind me. It may have the power to destroy me but it does not have the authority.

God gave permission for the enemy to give Job some of the worst tests of his life but He did not give the enemy the authority to destroy his life. Job, too, was in a faith fight. I must fight till the finish, trusting God all the way, come what may, reminding myself of the result of God's promise to me ... I win.

In my bathroom I have word art on my wall that states, "The Lord is my Strength and my Song," taken from Psalms 118:14. In my faith walk God has been giving me songs that help and guide me through my tough times. Songs that I have sang before but now have a new meaning. In my season of my faith fight, God reminded me of a song I use to sing, "Faith that can Conquer Anything," by Vanessa Bell Armstrong. I must maintain trust God even in things I don't understand. Faith when nothing else makes sense, not just faith the grain of a mustard seed but my faith has to be like when you are baking a cake. You can't see the inside of the cake being baked but you can smell it. My faith has to be able to smell faith during the fight. God has given me all the ingredients. I have to have faith until the end. I must continue maintain my faith to fight to the finish.

"Faith That Can Conquer Anything"

By Vanessa Bell Armstrong

I HAVE THE FAITH, THAT SEES THE

INVISIBLE, EXPECTS THE INCREDIBLE

RECEIVES THE IMPOSSIBLE FAITH, THAT

CAN CONQUER ANYTHING FAITH, THAT

UPROOTS MY PROBLEMS, FAITH, TO

KNOW GOD CAN SOLVE THEM FAITH, TO

VISION MY FREEDOM I HAVE FAITH, THAT

CAN CONQUER ANYTHING FAITH, TO

REACH THE UNREACHABLE, FAITH, TO

FIGHT THE UNBEATABLE FAITH, TO

REMOVE THE UNMOVABLE, FAITH, THAT

STANDS THE INVINCIBLE FAITH, THAT CAN

CONQUER ANYTHING

CHAPTER NINE

"The Silence"

Kenshalene Minott

As a child, I learned often from my environment that certain topics could not be discussed, nor did I receive a clear answer while families including the community held secrets. Could you imagine being approximately 10 years of age and asking life questions only to hear "just don't do it". Could you imagine growing up navigating through life having to figure out matters for yourself? Remember this, that the cycle of silence must be broken in order to become free. I hope this message will reach the young, teens, adults, and the elderly to stop having to experience bought lessons and to break the cycle of SILENCE.

Part 1-SILENCE

On my quest to becoming complete (whole), I learned that Silence has consequences. Silence indirectly shapes our **Perspective**; **Prevents** us from developing harmonies relationships; we become **Polluted** thus affecting others that are connected to us; and we develop a mind-set of being **Private**.

PERSPECTIVE-

Many women, children, and men have experienced trauma or abuse during their childhood. Abuse can be mental (manipulation), verbal, and physical. Trauma is the weight we carry after an event takes place and leaves an individual disturbed and hurting. The day I was abused, I remember it clear as day. My mother and brother went to the grocery store, while I was left alone with my mother's boyfriend, at that time. He started talking to me about boys; did I like any boys; and had I ever had sex with a boy. I shared with him how I liked boys but hadn't been with any one. He than began to share how if I wanted to be good at sex that he would need to teach me. At the age of 12, I was naïve to what it was leading to. After he had performed oral sex, I felt shamed and robbed of what was designed to be sacred (my body). My environment demonstrated that having different partners was normal, so keeping silent on matters that I knew were wrong I could not discuss. Keeping silent reinforced me in suppressing my feelings that consequently turned into isolation from my peers and family. The trauma that I experienced with this person created emotional and physical scaring on many levels. The trauma negatively shaped how I perceived myself and others. When our perspective has been distorted, it leads to low self-esteem and lies about ourselves appear to be true. If you compound lies, people casting you away with their words and not being filed with the Holy Spirit; you have an internal war going on in the inside of your mind, body and spirit. When we don't deal with this internal war, we carry this into adulthood. Now you have children and adults walking around broken. Don't think that keeping silent is only for the abused; its not. Denial perpetrates a cycle of negative perception, by thinking "If I ignore the problem somehow things will get better". It only gets better by being honest that something is wrong, talking it through, and then asking our creator to heal us. The misconception is thinking that only our hearts need healing, but I found to often it's the thoughts that are connected to our emotions that need to be healed. Talking with a previous client, she shared an event that lead to DV (domestic violence) and the way she described it was as if she was living in that very moment. For her, it happened over five years ago.

Who can save us? It's a simply answer…Jesus!

Jeremiah 30:17 says "For I will restore health unto you, and I will heal you of thy wounds, saith the Lord; because they called you an Outcast, saying this is Zion whom no man seeketh after". The beauty is that Gods word is full of how our Father see us, examples, and promises.

PREVENTION-

Let me start off by saying that prevention comes easy by accepting that a situation or event was out of your hands, forgiving, and getting past people false judgment of you. This sounds so easy right? Wrong! It's a process! One thing that I observe and experience that families care so much about is their reputation. Holding on to reputation can cripple an individual. For me, it was my elders not having information and having a form of godliness but not demonstrating the power that they sing nor heard about on Sunday. Since no one talked about matters that could save someone from repeating some of their mistakes, the results showed up in their children. So, I hid behind my brokenness. Thinking my issues of my past would somehow correct themselves. That was the lie the enemy wanted me to believe. Shut my mouth; never share to your child nor anyone. What lie have you been believing? The truth is, that when we open-up, fear must go.

Feeling intimidated by what we think people may say, will go. This allows God to arise and save our seed and generations coming after us to walk in freedom. **Is. 60:1 "Arise, shine; for thy light is come, and the glory of the LORD is risen upon thee"**. Our children need to know about sins that have been strong in our past generations and our lives so if something present itself to them, they are aware and not ignorant.

Here are some steps to prevention:

- Be honest to yourself of the things that hurt you.

- Pray God's word over yourself and your children. Ask

for the Lord to deliver you from iniquity (that sense of guilt) and presumptuous sin (things that you done that you were unaware that it caused you to error). **Psalm 51.**

- Listen to yourself. If somethings is wrong; it's wrong! Speak up!

- Put forth the effort in learning about your family issues. To stop the cycle from occurring to the next generation. The enemy would love for us to stay ignorant. By devoting yourself to spending time in reading the Word of God will build up your confidence. **Proverbs 3:26 "For the LORD shall be thy confidence and shall keep thy foot from being taken".**

- Set aside your need to be liked. Are you struggling with the fear of people accepting you or scared of being rejected?

- Talk about it. For me it was talking it through with my spouse.

- Cry out to God! A lot of times, people don't even know that they are in a bad state.

- If you start seeing a change in your child, teen, or an adult behavior that is not normal/not themselves; behavior become attention seeker (going to the doctor a lot, not wanting to go to school, or church) start probing; asking questions. Don't ignore the signs.

- Consider what type of environment you want your children to be around. The greatest prevention is watching the type of environment that you place your child in.

Remember this, that your identity is not based upon the person who wronged you or violated you. It's because of Sin that situations had occurred. You're not at fault. Secondly, it is the parent job to protect the child. Therefore, parents including me, in order to close the door to whatever had you weighed down, depressed, feeling alone and so forth…. pursue God with all you have! Tell your flesh "you will line up with God's word"! Jesus says in **Hebrew 11:6 "No one can please**

God without faith, for whoever comes to God must have faith that God exists and rewards those who seek him" GNT.

POLLUTON/PRIVATE-

If you or I are not careful, hurt can turn into toxin. When we don't deal with issues, pollution turns to this: defiance, anger, bitter, shame, guilt, empty, isolation, pride, low self-worth, and more. Then we kick in to survival mode. Survival mode is trying to mentally tell yourself "I got to fake it; can't let nobody see me for who I am'. I did this for years. To the point that I became numb in arears that God did not design for me to be. Its funny how when we let stuff go on and on, we become desensitize to that feeling or emotion. Oppression came in when I tried to manage all these negative feelings and thoughts on my own. Then I began seeking love in men who were damaged and broken. Friends, sisters, and brothers, if we sweep secrets under the rug (an old saying), the victim is left with a scar while others move on with their lives.

When I began my journey to wholeness, I first held on to Hope. The first compliment I received was from my father. He said "Ken,

Ken you are beautiful the way you are". That was a seed of affirmation and love planted that I held on to. Secondly, one day in a church service a good friend that I served in ministry said to me "I'm not able to pray for you at this moment but I encourage you to go to the altar for prayer and ask to be delivered from all the men you had been sexually connected to". Then she went on to say, "then after God cleanses you, ask God to hide you; and that the man that He designs for you will find you". That night was a life changing moment for me. I then allowed God to minister to the little girl inside. Jesus began to show me a genuine love that was not artificial; not counterfeit; and to love myself. Psalm 139:14

(MSG) "I thank you, High God - you're breathtaking! Body and soul, I am marvelously made! I worship in adoration - what a creation"!

MATTHEW 11:28-29

"Come unto me, all ye that are labour and are heavy laden, and I will give you rest.

Take my yoke upon you and learn of me; for I am meek and lowly in heart: and ye shall find rest unto your souls".

Once Jesus comes in, you don't feel a disconnect. A disconnect between about yourself and life. See when we are private about matters that are happening in our home, we lose that sense of being content. We find ourselves putting forth extra energy in trying to cover up what we lack and consequently it indirectly affects the people who are close to us. Isolation robs you from having peace and developing harmonies relationships with others. Jesus is not a God who is tied to a name nor our status nor our money. His will for all of us is to be saved! By allowing myself to become vulnerable, it sent Jesus an invitation to totally cleanse the pollution and change my perspective. When that enemy called "deception" has been illuminated by the power of God's Word; information, awareness, and a level of maturity arises. **Psalm 68:1 "Let God arise, let his enemies be scattered...". What is your enemy?** One enemy that will be scattered is the mind set of having short term relationships. See the enemy wants hurt or trauma to cripple you from obtaining and maintaining long-term relationships. For when you come to the mind-set of long-term relationship the way you treat God will be the way you treat and respond to people. Let me break this down; those that have a short-term relationship mentality are on and off when it comes down to their devotion with God and attitude towards people. I call that a "Wonderer" mentality. I had a "Wonderer" mentality for many years. I found myself in and out of relationships and unstable. I was just being a survivor and not thriving. Jesus desires long-term relationships and consistency. The results will be evident, and you will begin to abide and remain in his presence and enjoy the fullness of joy. When that light bulb comes on my sisters and friends, you won't second guess if you have been set-free; you will have the confidence that the power of the Holy Spirit has transformed your heart; your mind; your ways; your walk, your talk; your lenses. Everything is possible to those that have faith!

In closing, once you decide to reject the state of being silent, and you begin to let the Lord help you. God will affirm you. God will in still his goodness. If you allow him to change your heart and your hurt, you will see results. If people start opposing you for being honest and prevent your healing, God will supply you the contentment and affirmation on who you are. So, don't every second guess the new journey. God will begin a new work in you, and you will live in His Glory and newness. As you began to discover and unfold the layers of hurt, know that you are not alone. We are blessed now to gain information and awareness through other stories and testimonies. After reading this, areas of your life are starting to shift for you now! God wants the best for you; it is his desire for cycles not to continue to go on and that the enemy be exposed. The lies of the enemy begin to be rejected and cast down. The guilt, shame and regret that has lingered for years begin to be replaced with goodness, mercy and praise. I declare **Psalm 112:2 "His seed shall be mighty upon the earth: the generation of the upright shall be blessed". Thank you, Jesus, for the SHIFT!** Change starts with you.

CHAPTER TEN

"Be Fabulous & Forgive"

Apollonia Ellis

"Family is supposed to be our safe-haven. Very often, it's the place where we find the deepest heartache" (Iyanla Vazant). A-P-O-L-L-O-N-I-A, I was 4-years-old when I learned how to spell my name, my grandmother did everything she could to teach me to spell it; she was adamant about me being prepared for preschool. At that age, my Grandmother was really "Momma" to me.

Although my grandmother says that I lived with my mother for a short period of time, that memory seems to sit somewhere in the back of my mind, and I haven't been able to locate it. For as far back as I can remember, I was always my grandmother's baby. When she would prepare to leave the house, I would watch her scrupulously, as she went to grab her purse and keys, I always knew then, it was my time to head to the door. If I didn't leave with her, she knew that it would be just like going to war because I was not letting her leave the house without me! I never wanted my grandmother to leave.

I was always this overly independent child. I would always be the first to wake up in the mornings between me and my sisters, especially the day after grocery shopping, so that I could be the one to choose which box of cereal would get opened first. One of my grandmother's rules was that only one box of cereal could be open at a time. I would push a chair up to the counter, jump on the chair to get onto the counter, all to get a bowl out the cabinet and the cereal off the top of the refrigerator. Sometimes the milk would be a brand-new gallon which would make the gallon heavy and cause me to make a spill when pouring the milk into the bowl. I would try to clean it up the best way a 4-year-old could!

As a kid, I could always remember watching television shows and movies and they would have; children, a loving mother and a working father. So, a lot of times my thoughts would be, "Why don't I have my mother," or "Why do I live with my grandmother and not my mother and father". A mother popping up every now and then, was the reality of what I had as a mother. When my grandmother would go out of town for trips, my mother would baby sit us while she was gone. Those were the times I got to feel just a little dose of what it was to have your mother. She would braid my hair, it would be so tight that my neck couldn't bend. I would leave whatever style she did in my head, probably until the next time she came over.

Going to the park with your mom, your mom picking you up from school and you running up and giving her a big hug, or just having a nice time under the sun with your mom were only things I was able to dream about as a kid. Those were things I would only get to experience by playing with my dolls and pretending they were mother and daughter. My only actual encounter of a mom was her bringing us money to go skating with our church at the time, to only come back late that night knocking on the window and asking for the money back. She promised she would bring the money back to us the next day, which she did, minutes before the church bus came to pick us up.

I can remember several times when my mother would go to rehab. She would come home sober for a couple months, walking around with a Bible in one hand. I'd think to myself, "Maybe this will be the time it really lasts" and "Maybe this time my sisters and I will get to finally have our mother", but those just remained thoughts that never became reality. Shortly after it would be back to the streets and drugs. At that time, I didn't understand the severity of having an addiction; my feelings would be so hurt just thinking that not one of her four daughters were worth her giving up her addiction. How could drugs come before your children? As I grew older, I learned that addiction is powerful, and my mom was one of the victims of falling into the likes of crack cocaine. Which at the time, I later learned, was in its prime.

My grandmother did her best to raise my four sisters and I. Being that she was only 13 when she birthed her first child, which is my late aunt, and birthed my mother shortly after. She basically learned on her own how to be a parent; later on having to take on the task of raising her four granddaughters. Although she may have had other jobs along the way, the one I mostly remember was her being a bus driver. My grandmother always loved to drive. I remember trips with her driving to Mississippi, my sisters and I crammed in the back seat. Life with Grandma at that time was good! Especially for a kid. We did different things and went to different events. I would be happy at those moments, but always in the back of my mind, I wanted my mother.

Grandma would have us at the dining room table having conversations as if we had the option to soon live with our mother. After several sit-downs and it never happened, I gave up on that hope. Christmas was one of my favorite holidays because that's when I knew Grandma would have one of her big holiday parties and I was for sure to see my mom. But then those memories became sour because the night would always end up with her arguing and fighting with somebody at the party, most of the time it would be with whatever guy she was dating at the time. She would sometimes leave without even acknowledging us, so then I started trying to figure out, "What can I do to make my mother want me". I started growing hate in my heart towards her, but I didn't want that because I knew it wasn't God-like. Growing up, no matter what, God was always our foundation, so I would always pray to him to remove the hate in my heart the bitterness of not having my mother.

I then started trying to participate in programs at school. I'd see other students' mothers, fathers and grandparents coming to support them. I thought for sure that if I started participating in the school choir and doing good academically that my mother would be proud and would come to the school to support me! Program after program, award after award, honor roll on top of honor roll; not one appearance from my mother. I inwardly had feelings of still not being good enough, which made me want to work even harder. Then I started to form this attitude of wanting to be an overachiever and wanting to be unique from everyone else which was followed by years of me being an honors student and years of me accomplishing many coveted titles and positions as a young leader. I'd think, "There has got to be something that will one day get my mother's attention." All thoughts, but never my reality.

Time had gone by and my sisters and I moved from foster home to foster home after being a witness of sexual molestation. At the time I did what I was told, and I thought I had done the right thing, but shortly after I told what I had witnessed with my own eyes, we were taken away from my grandmother's home which then caused us to be away from our grandmother. Imagine a child, a little girl, already yearning the love and attention from her mother; her grandmother trying her best to fulfill that void; and now the grandmother is taken away.

My sisters and I were split up into two foster homes, the older two in one home and the younger two in another. The younger two would be and my sister that was next to me in age. The foster home we lived in could very much be compared to kid jail. We were treated as if we did something wrong, as if it were our fault that we were in the foster home. I don't remember the foster mom's name to this day, because she forced us to call her MOM. If we didn't call her "Mom" then it would be a harsh punishment behind it.

All I can remember was going to school, coming home, cleaning up, taking a nap, cleaning up, taking another nap, cleaning up and eating toward the end of the evening. We couldn't drink anything after 6pm, so my sister and I would use our hands to sneak water when we would pretend to have to use the restroom. My sister and I would have talks with each other when we had to take a nap, but most of the time they would try to keep us separated. If you were caught talking during nap time, then that meant a beating from her husband in the brown suit with the big black belt. That's all I remember of him and that's the only time I ever saw him.

Those people should not have been foster parents. We were able to visit our grandmother from time to time, and the departures from those visits were terrible memories. Me screaming and yelling wanting to stay with my grandmother. The lady with the long bang in the back, and the short hair at the top, very skinny, was in my head as a monster. Who would want to take kids away from their loved ones? I did what I was told to do, at that moment I started to wish I wouldn't have said anything and just kept it to myself, maybe then we would still be living with our grandmother. That is when I started to form a hate towards older men, because had he not did what he did, then we wouldn't be in the position we were in. I formed hate in my heart for a long time towards him and towards my mother, because I felt she should've been the one protecting us.

My prayers to God had one day been answered when the lady that I looked upon as a monster, then turned into an angel when she took us to our grandmother's house and told us she was not coming back this time to get us, that we were home for good! Life would go back to normal, so I thought, but all my sisters didn't return home. I then begin to wonder why, was it because of me? My sister started making visits as sparsely as my mom did. I didn't know what was going on with her, all I knew was that there was another person vaguely gone from my life.

My grandmother had begun to get sick and my sisters and I had started growing older, becoming teenagers and wanting to do teenager things. We started being rebellious, not following any of the rules. My grandmother was not in good enough health at the time to discipline us. We all grew up faster than we should, but that part was from our own account. My grandmother did the best she could, while my mother was somewhere enjoying her life, she may have had 99 problems, but her children weren't one.

As a teenager, I saw the relationships my friends had with their mothers and I became close with some of their mom's, going to them for advice and just getting motherly love from them. God sent many women in my life as mother figures, but the problem was, it was always just that, a "Mother-Figure" and never "MY MOTHER". I always said to myself, "When I have children, I'll never abandon them." That feeling can be one of the worst feelings, especially when it comes from your own mother. At that time, I again prayed that God would put forgiveness in my heart for my mother.

My mother finally became sober when I was an adult! She remained sober for the longest she'd ever been in her life. My thoughts were now whether I'd have the mother I'd always wanted. Even though I was an adult, there was still hope in my heart. I felt like it was never too late to build a relationship with my mother, being that I had just found out who my biological father was when I was the age of 30. Now he and I have a great relationship; it's like I've known him all my life. So, I'm thinking now I can get this bond with my mother, then I will finally have a bond with my Mom and Dad! I know you can't make up for lost time, but you can start all over and build!

Reality finally set in when I realized that sober or not, my mother's intentions were not to have a relationship with me, in fact, not with any of her daughters. She had desires, but none of them were to build a relationship, a bond with her daughters or be there for her grandchildren. I never doubted that she loved us, but I've learned some people love themselves more than anything else, even their children.

I've concluded that there are some women who give birth to children and that's it, and there are others who give birth and actually care to raise their children. I vowed to myself to be the latter. I've always asked myself, "Why forgiveness? Why let it go? Why move-on, after what they've done?" Then I thought "Jesus forgave on Friday, and was resurrected on Sunday", I cannot afford to forfeit my russeruction, holding a grudge.

v. 14 For if you forgive other people when they sin against you, your heavenly Father will also forgive you **v. 15** But if you do not forgive others their sins, your Father will not forgive your sins.

(Matt.6:14-15 New Living Translation)

Forgiveness is not as easy as it sounds. I'm 34 and I'm just now at peace with the situation. I've learned you that you can dwell on situations that you cannot change. I've prayed and forgiven my mother, I love her with every piece of me and I can live with the fact that I may never have that relationship I want, but I thank God for the many mother-figure's he sent my way. Forgiveness will take you far. I no longer have any hate or bad feelings in my heart towards my mother. It's one thing to be fabulous on the outside, but it's a great thing to be fabulous on the INSIDE and have a forgiving heart. Forgiving others may help you more than the person your forgiving. That person in the past that may have caused you hurt in some sort of way, it only hurts you to hang on to it. BE FABULOUS AND FORGIVE!

CHAPTER ELEVEN

WHY ME? WHY NOT YOU?

BRUCINA L. MAYFIELD

To begin my story, I would be remiss to not share of simply how wonderful God has been in my life, to say the least. This story has been in the making since my time of birth. The moment I was placed in the womb of my mother and birthed into the earth, the name of Brucina Liawatha Mayfield was unique all its own. So many have asked, "Did your mother name you after your father Bruce?" Most would think that would be the case, however, my answer has always been, "No." My mother named me after Bruce Lee! My father's name is Charlie Mayfield to which of course, he also played a part in this whole becoming of me as well.

As many may know, the legend of Bruce Lee, being that of a Kung Fu fighting machine, he was one who never gave up and normally out-witted his opponents with fancy footwork, stamina, skill and mind power. I must be the first to admit that I may not have the fancy footwork, but I do credit my attributes to his stamina, skill and mind power that has accompanied me through many obstacles I've faced in life. For God hath not given me the spirit of fear; but of power, and of love, and of sound mind (2 Timothy 1:7). I truly believe in this scripture as it has carried me through many dark and lonely nights filled with tears.

At one era in my life, I thought that tears were all I knew and this was the only way to live; in my own misery. This journey I've been on has not been easy, just as many of the women who are a part of this testimonial book will attest and say, if it had not been for the grace and mercy of God, where would we be. I can't speak for anyone but myself, but I must say that I know I would be completely lost. There have been moments in my life that truly could have led a person to either lose their mind or possibly even take their own life.

Yes, take their own life! Which at one point and time I must admit, this was me. The date was November 8, 1997 and it was what I thought would be the beginning of my happily ever after. I had just embarked upon becoming newly married to a wonderful man who was the epitome of my happy during that era of my life. The ink was barely dry on our nuptials sealing that we had finally become one flesh under the eyesight of God, only to turn around four days later to be placed in the most daunting challenges of both of our young lives.

Many who live in Michigan know that there's this ugly thing called "black ice" and that if you aren't careful either walking or driving, something horrible may happen if safety measures aren't taken. On the morning of November 12, 1997, we got to the portion of your vows that state, "for better or for worse, in sickness and in health," right away.

That evening before on November 11, let's just say if you've been married and a newlywed, you can only imagine three days into your marriage... you're hopefully still on a high that only you and your spouse can feel. But the beginning of what happily ever after would feel like came to an abrupt stop. We traveled that evening to take his best man back to Lansing in hopes of simply returning the next morning to begin our future together, but that unfortunately was not the case.

Black ice is what met us at our humble beginnings to what we thought would be forever. We were involved in an almost fatal accident that basically could've taken both of our lives. But GOD!!! I can remember as the van we were driving in toppled, flipping repeatedly, I immediately grabbed the hand of my husband at the time and began crying on the name of Jesus, three times!!!! Instantly his hand was torn away from me and he was tossed to the back of the vehicle we were in. Not even being aware that I was in the world at that point, I still held on to the name of Jesus, as it was girded down within my faintest cry. At that moment, I truly believed God heard me and pitied my groan!

God spared both of our lives. However, I was left in a wheelchair paralyzed from the T6 vertebrae on down. Challenges as a young couple came and they went just as in any marriage. As we all know, to everything there is a season and a reason. As we grow in life and in and out of relationships, we know there are moments in time that can either make us or break us and unfortunately, we were broken as a couple. However, through God, 10 years were given to us as we tried to make those years work as best we could, considering the cards we had been dealt.

Earlier I mentioned that I was faced with of course many moments of depression, tears, and fears, to which I truly felt like giving up. So much so that I would ask the question, "God, why didn't you just end it all! What worth will I ever be living life from a wheelchair? What role would I play in life that would be of benefit, not only to myself but to others yet alone a husband?" I would plead to the Lord saying, "God, I come to you as humbly as I know how.

Why did you leave me like this? Why me?"

As sure as I asked that question, a resounding voice that startled me to the point of looking around in the room to see who was there with me said, "Why not you? I was spat upon, beaten, battered and bruised all for you; hung on a tree, pierced in the hands, feet and side; crown of thorns placed upon my head, all for you! So again, I ask Brucina, why not you?" "The cross you will bear will not be an easy one, but as I stated above, stamina, skill and brain power have all been a part of the blueprint to life given to you from the time of your conception."

My work on earth was not finished. The morning of November 12, 1997, He wasn't ready for me yet. There was yet and still life that I had to live. Facing yet more obstacles to come; another marriage to which I placed my all into, however to once again fail, seemed to be my plight. This time in that failed moment, there was yet another lesson that had to be learned.

I didn't go into questioning God as to why, yet another heartache had befallen me, but counted it all joy even during my tears. Those tears shed would further build my resume and true testimony on life to validate that in that season, the reason for it all would soon manifest itself and its purpose for being.

"Keep it ta movin," at this point and time had become the motto that I established for myself. Regardless of what blows I'd been dealt in life through my pain, broken-heart and let downs, there was yet and still a testimony being built that would one day give birth too; one day I'd have to push. What I've come to learn of myself out of all the relationships that I've encountered is to face the fact that I'd given more to others than I'd given to myself. I'd encountered relationship after relationship only to be taken advantage of, all because of my giving heart.

After yet another failed marriage then on to another failed attempt at a relationship that I should have known was not of God, I tried because I saw something in someone that he didn't even see in himself. I'd come to terms with a statement that my best friend of over 38 years quoted to me, "No more Detours." How many times in life have we been on a path in our lives that we thought we were truly heading in the right direction to end up having to make either a U-turn or simply turn all the way back around to start at our very beginning?

The blueprint of our very existence would be considered our starting point that begins and ends with our creator. Truly, I've accepted each bump in the road that they were all set ups to who God intended on me to become this very day. Some look at me and wonder how do you keep going? What drives you to not give up? Why are you even working and going to school? Why? Why? Why? My response just as God spoke so clearly to me at the beginning of all this 21 years ago, "Why not me?"

This journey has not been an easy one. However, there's some little girl, some young lady or possibly even some mother on the mother's board that needs to see what strength in the face of adversity looks like. The strength that allows a woman to get up each morning, with her body aching with pains, mind filled with fears of what's to come or even possibly feeling as though life has been sucked out of you to the place of unrecognition. BUT GOD! God sees us ladies. He sees who we are striving to become and even more importantly, who we belong too.

God has implanted inside each one of us the willpower to make sound and wise decisions, not just for ourselves but for our families as well. But first, just as I had to learn through all the hardships I've experienced in life, I had to come to terms with self; learning of my own self-reliance and worth. How can you truly give love away when you're not fully in love with yourself? When you learn to love on you and realize truly just what you will accept and not accept in your life is when you will come in full view of the woman you look at in the mirror daily.

At one point in my life I didn't like the person I saw each day. I lost her all for the sake of trying to help someone else see themselves, which became an ever-losing battle. As that person fought their own battles, I unknowingly was losing my own fight. First Lady Trina propositioned me with this opportunity several times as she saw something in me that I wasn't even seeing within myself. I was in a cloud. A cloud of self-doubt and pity, thinking to myself who would want to listen to my story, all while yet living outside of what God purposed for me at the time of my accident.

Although First Lady Trina wanted me to come forth with my testimony, my story had not come to its full formation. I yet and still had to go through another set-back to be set up to give birth to this ever-growing spiritual baby that had been growing inside of me. It's now time for me to push. Truly, this is my season to open my mouth and say something! God has been coddling me, protecting me and growing me to the place I've now come to.

My spiritual baby is no longer a baby that needs to be birthed into the atmosphere, my baby, that is, my testimony, is now 21 years old and God is calling her to come forth. I've been in this chair 21 years of my life and I can finally say my shift season has come! My winning season has arrived and I'm giving birth to what my destiny looks like from this time forth. I am no longer allowing myself to be a victim of mind manipulation or being made to feel as though I don't matter, all for the sake of someone else's downfalls.

My mission and purpose in life is to share with others that we, as women, have to forever stay in the fight. We must fight through our tears of heartbreak, moments of feeling as though we don't amount to anything, depression, setbacks, job loss, children going on their wayward way or possibly even the loss of a loved one. Surely, the pain of that alone may cause a person to lose faith. Just know that we all must trust God's word knowing that by having mustard seed faith we can develop a true BUT GOD testimony.

I've declared for this new year, and the rest of my life, that I will win!!! I'll be a champion if for no one else, myself. When you finally declare and decree that enough is enough, you develop a spirit of triumph and victory that truly belongs to you no matter the cost. Develop a mentality that you are priceless, no longer allowing yourself to feel worthless and by all cost, the world shall know this because you believe it as well.

This blessed opportunity to write this chapter is a tribute to all the women in my life who have encouraged me, rooting for me every step of the way, or should I say, every roll of the way. Most of them telling me that I am truly an inspiration to them for all I've endured and still, I am yet able to say I have victory in Jesus. To you ladies, each one of you, allow me to let you in on a little secret... I've rooted for you and cheered you on also. Through every word you've shared with me to boost me, please know that I've done the same for you through prayer and supplication to God on each of your behalf.

In my closing, I want to thank you Lady Trina, for seeing me when I couldn't even see myself. But most importantly, God saw me and has made me into who I've become today all because I trusted him as He trusted me. I look forward to this journey that I've been placed on. I pray to God for the spirit of boldness that will allow me to no longer remain quiet, but to come forth with a mighty lioness roar.

One of my hidden treasures that God has given me is the ability to write poems. This poem I choose to share is one that fits perfectly for this season that I'm in and was written in 2016 entitled "I'm Pregnant." Please take a moment and allow these words to transcend into your spirit as it did for me.

"I'm Pregnant!"

Each contraction is only a distraction making it hard to concentrate;

As I continue to debate with self

Searching and seeking for wealth of my own mind pulling to find

My destiny the place my God has promised me Give birth, do it now, find some way, any way Somehow!

To give way to this birth as you continue finding your worth More precious than diamond rings

This birth you have in your belly has a deep meaning It must be shared

It must be seen Not just for you

But for someone else's inner being

The power you have is not just in your songs

The power you preserve will allow so many to Overcome!

Give birth

You're pregnant, not in the natural man's eye

But your pregnancy will give way to the beginning and unleashing of so many Lives…..

PUSH…….She's here!!!!!

Brucina, 2016

CHAPTER TWELVE

WAR ROOM NOTES

NAKIA MOODY

"Father of the fatherless and protector of the widows, is God in his holy habitation"

– Psalm 68:5

God said, I will be a father to the fatherless. When I repeat this over and over again in my head, I reflect on the many struggles, burdens, heartaches, loneliness, and hatred I had in my heart. All the pain I kept inside because I couldn't grasp what God was trying to tell me. I didn't realize he was telling me not to worry because *he* was my father above all earthly fathers given. Even above the fathers of my children-the ones who said they would be there and help me through everything then left before things even had the chance to get tough. It was God who led me to them and God who placed them in my life.

These are issues that I've struggled with because I have not been able to see what good they are providing to me or my children.

As I work on building my relationship and finding my way back to God, I understand I must first come to terms with the decisions I've made, and the consequences along with them. I didn't grow up acting older than I should or hanging out with a lot of "street" friends. I was naïve to many things happening in the world because I was sheltered. Growing up, I remember my dad was always in the streets. Always juggling women, and when I was with him, I was always along for the ride. He would take me to these different women houses and I would watch him as each woman would cook for him, give him money and anything he wanted. He would leave me on the couch to watch television and would disappear for hours in a room with them. Now that I'm older, I realize he left me sitting there to go have sex with these women. This happened anytime I was with him. Sometimes he would drop me off with them and I would miss school because he wouldn't come back to get me. I remember days being left at school because he would be so busy with his women that he would forget to pick me up. He would always tell me that he loved me and that it would never happen again. Of course, I believed him because he was my dad and I loved him so much; and of course, it happened again.

I have always had an issue with feeling like I was never good enough for my dad. I remember him spending lots of time with my brothers and sisters who had a different father or children of the women he was seeing but leaving nearly any time for me. It was like I wasn't even there. I would wait for hours upon hours for him to pick me up. Staring out the window looking at every car that would whiz by, hoping that the next one would be his. He never showed up. How can a father tell a child they are "on their way" to get them and never make it to them? How can you have a child sitting, and missing their day ???waiting on you to show up when you know you never had any intention on ever going to get them? I remember, one day, stopping by the candy store on the way home. As I approached the store I could see that my dad was inside. This made me excited and I rushed to get in the store, only to find him gone. Nowhere to be found. He hid from me! My own father went and hid somewhere so that he didn't have to see me. What did I do to make him hate me so much, I thought. I cried all the way home, but bottled it up and never told my mom. From then on, I'd made up my mind that there was no way he could possibly love me. He just couldn't.

I would ask God why I had to have the dad that didn't show up to graduation, talent shows, or conferences, or anything that I had going on. The hurt cause by my toxic relationship with my father led me to toxic relationships with other men. I became accepting of the love they decided they wanted me to have. I accepted the lies, deceit, and repeated apologies. I forgave time after time because that's what I always did with my dad-forgave him and forgot. How could I grow up to be confident knowing woman when most of the hurt I've received by men came from my dad? I remember him telling me I would never get a boyfriend because of the way I looked. He said I didn't look like the smaller girls and was too big for anyone to want to be with me. That was the beginning of my self-hate. This only worsened when my dad had a bi-racial child. He loved and doted on that boy so much, you would have thought he gave birth to him himself! I had no idea my dad was capable of this kind of love because he'd never shown it to me or anyone else, for that matter.

I became vulnerable, looking for love any way I could find it and taking it from anyone who would give it. I became sexually active at a young age thinking that having sex meant the person loved me. I thought this way because no one ever told me that was foolish thinking or that guys will tell you whatever you want to hear just to get what they want from you. Although I was older, on the inside I was still that same little girl longing for love and affection from a father who wasn't there. The first time I had sex I felt terrible afterwards. I immediately regretted my decision and wished I had waited. I was pressured into doing something that I wasn't ready for all because he wanted a 'virgin'. I was left with this empty feeling all the while his ego had been stroked. I remember walking home in pain and crying on the inside because I knew it was something I could never take back. I had no one to talk to about this because I should've "known better". I let him groom me into a fool and it all went downhill from there.

When I met my oldest son's father I was out with my cousin hanging around boys. You know, doing things I should not have been doing, but trying to fit in. In no time, I was hooked on him and then I found myself pregnant right out of high school. I became a mother in the blink of an eye. No senior prom, no graduation, open house, pictures, or parties. Just parenthood. I wasn't prepared for the life I was going to have with him. I was still young and naïve and now more than ever, I wanted my relationship to work and willing to do anything to prove it could. In doing so, I spent years dealing with physical abuse, depression, anxiety, sexually transmitted diseases-that he passed to me from other women-lies, hurt, and countless women that he would bring in our home and sleep with. Through all of this I decided to stay. Listening to his apologies, repeated affirmations of love and foolishly believing everything that he would tell me. Once again accepting the love he was willing to give me, only now realizing it wasn't love at all. It was control. I remember crying one night while he was getting ready to go out. I cried because I knew he was going to be with another woman. As I was crying, he grabbed my face and started laughing at me and said, "you alright," and left. It was in that moment I vowed never to cry in front of a man again. As I grew detached, the fights increased. I don't know if he thought he was losing me so he had to beat me into submission, or what, but I remember being choked so bad with the back of my neck on the curb that my throat bent inward. That was painful, but what was more painful was my sister sitting on her front porch watching it happen and doing nothing. There was a time that he punched me in my face so hard that he knocked me out and fractured my jaw. Crying and looking at myself in the mirror I just kept wondering what I did to deserve all of this. I started to catch him out with different females that he would stay with for days at a time. God gave me outlets, but I did not take them. When I finally did, I was damaged beyond repair.

I completely lost myself and turned into someone I no longer knew. My heart became cold, and I started spiraling out of control. Covering the pain with alcohol and sex, 'Nakia' was gone and I'd become 'NeNe'. Although I lived a double life, I was still a great parent. But at night and when my son was away, I would lose myself in men, drugs, and alcohol. Everything I envisioned for myself became a dream that happened only when I slept because all the different men became my reality. They were like the air I breathed; they were what sustained me. I once wanted to become a probation office and I saw those dreams dashed from me, but that's fine. It's not until you lose everything, that you realize what you could have had. Once people started noticing my choices, I started getting a lot of 'why' from them. It's useless trying to explain something to someone that has not been through your struggle. Someone who has a home and love and can't comprehend that you're seeking those things in other people. I've always been an 'unusual' girl, my mother described me as, "a chameleon girl with no moral compass to north, no fixed personality, just an inner indecisiveness that was as wide and wavery as the ocean." Wow, right? But if I were to say I didn't see my life ending up this way, it would be a lie. I was born to be the *other* woman, not *the* woman. I belonged to no one who belonged to everyone. I had nothing but wanted everything. With a fire for every experience and a passion for freedom that terrified me to the point of never speaking about it. What I was trying to fill was something that I didn't realize only God could fill, only God could heal. My brother would pray and cry with me, he sat me down and said, "Nakia, a woman is supposed to love and be love. I've been watching you and see the way you've been handling men. You're treating them like they're women-like they're disposable. I know you're hurt, but you can't continue to be like this." God spoke to me through my brother and let me know that I am capable of being loved. I was tired of living the life I had.

"Then Jesus said to his disciples, if anyone wishes to come after me, he must deny himself and take up his cross and follow me." – Matthew 16:20

I started having withdrawals. I wanted to be with a man so bad that I would lock myself in the bathroom and rock back and forth cradling my knees to my chest. All I could do was pray that God would get me through this. He did! But in his deliverance, I found myself in another toxic relationship. I fell into a deep depression, left one bad relationship and ended up pregnant and in another one. This relationship was much like the same and I ended up having a miscarriage. I lost what I believed to be my first baby girl. I will never get over having to grab the baby and the sack out of the toilet and taking it to the hospital and once again being alone. He was nowhere to be found but made every excuse as to why he couldn't be there. I remained quiet. Zoned out for days, as I couldn't eat or sleep because I was so hurt. I just cried and cried thinking to myself, 'this man killed my baby. He's the reason my child is not here'. All the crying, fighting, stressing, having guns pulled on me, and just non-stop stress dealing with him.

I kept hearing something telling me to go home, and I was ignoring it. I remember receiving three messages from three different people telling me to go home, but I kept ignoring them. One morning while heading home to get ready for a potential job interview, I started to feel like something heavy was weighing me down. The closer I got to my exit the more light-headed I became. I turned the radio up, rolled down the windows, and slowed my speed to try to gain control of the situation. I was one exit away and my vision turned black. The next thing I remembered was someone asking me if I was OK. I'd blacked out while driving. The devil was really trying to kill me! But God, he wasn't ready for me to go! I was told, had I not slowed down, I would have flown through my windshield and landed on the other side of the highway in incoming traffic. My car crushed into the median and all I had left was the back doors.

Everything was crushed, my head went into the windshield, I broke a few teeth, my legs were cut open, and all my teeth went through my tongue. But I was alive! However, I looked and felt horrible. I didn't want to go outside, and I lost everything. I mean I was left with nothing. My boyfriend left me because I was no longer an asset to him. I didn't have anything so he didn't want me. I finally packed up and went home. I went home with nothing, not even a pair of shoes. I was wearing sandals in the dead of winter. One person came to me and gave me money to get a pair of shoes because she couldn't stand to see me like that. In that time, God showed me who was really in my life to help. This was my chance to start over, so I did. As time went on, I was in a better place in my life. I was working, I purchased another vehicle, had money coming in, and was starting my life with me and my son. Things had started to look up for us.

I met a guy not intending to meet anyone, but just speaking to him here and there. Finally, I gave him my phone number and we started texting, then we met up and from that night on, became inseparable. We were seeing each other every day, enjoyed laughing and joking around with one another, started going on dates, then started having sex. He would come to my job almost every day, we talked or would text every day, all day. I thought God had finally sent me the person that I was going to be with forever. I was blinded by the things he did that no other guy had done that I didn't realize when the relationship became toxic. By that time, it was hard to get away. I started finding out about all the other girls he was involved with, and I started accepting the same behavior I did from previous relationships. I was believing his lies and that he loved me, not realizing that he just loved the convenience of me. The fact that I took care of business, he could trust me, I had my own place, cooked, cleaned, I was a clean person, and nurturing. I thought all those things mattered until I realized the girls he was cheating on me with, were the complete opposite! Very nasty, unclean girls. Yet, I still didn't pay attention to the signs. By the time I could see the red flags I was in too deep. Finally, we decided to go our separate ways, and I became the old person I was. I started having sex with a guy I knew. I used sex to fill a void. As time went on, I knew something wasn't right and found out I was pregnant. I went to the doctor to confirm and to find out how far along I was. The time didn't match up with the other guy I was dating, so I informed the other guy. That was the worst nine months I've ever been through in my life. He came around when the baby was months old. By myself, lonely, and just too hurt to even smile. He was living across from my apartment with another girl and wanted nothing to do with me. With all my heart I knew the child was his. He had doubts, but I wanted to assure the child was his so we took an at home paternity test. The test came back that he was 99.9999% NOT the father. That took me down to pieces and I know it tore him down as well. This child that he had built a bond with was not his. We still tried to work through it, but he became abusive. I felt so bad, I started to feel like I deserved it. No matter how much I apologized, nothing I ever did was good enough. It took time for me to understand that although I did something wrong, I couldn't keep letting him punish me for it. I was on pins and needles around him, always scared to say anything wrong. He would get upset anytime I went out with friends or family and would tell me things he heard them saying about my business so that I would get upset with them and not be around them anymore. It made me close myself off to everyone-friends and family, I just wanted to be alone. It was fine because they didn't want to be in his presence anyway. He would sit outside drinking then come in the house and accuse me of just getting off the phone with a guy or talking to someone. When his kids would come visit, he would have them constantly watching me and reporting to him what I was doing. If I was taking a nap, I was being accused of being tired because I was sleeping around. I had no peace in my own home. He would want to stay on the phone while I was at work to see if I was working with guys. Meanwhile, he was texting females telling them what he wanted to do to them and inviting them to my house while I was at work. God gave me every reason to leave, and I found every reason to stay; thinking I could change him.

"Now devote your heart and soul to seeking the LORD your God. Begin to build the sanctuary of the LORD God, so that you may bring the ark of the covenant of the LORD and the sacred articles

belonging to God into the temple that will be built for the Name of the LORD." - 1 Chronicles 22:18

That was the furthest thing from what he wanted to do when he knew I was hurting. He wanted to build a foundation with God but didn't believe in God unless something went wrong. My home was the Devil's playground. I called my home 'The hell house', after everything that was happening. Being pregnant, being pushed to the ground, punched in the face, showing up to work with busted lips, and bruises on my body. My coworkers were looking at me with concern, but not knowing what to say. There were nights I would have to pull my lips out of my braces from being punched in the face. Scared, and on the couch holding my children while he sits on the other end of the couch holding a gun. There were nights sitting in my car screaming crying because I was tired of being harassed all while he stood outside my car. I felt trapped.

He would leave suicide notes stating he wanted to kill himself, threaten to kill me and my children then himself. I had no one to turn to. I would hear, "leave him", but I wanted him to be better. I wasn't thinking of myself or my children. It was an emotional roller-coaster. I prayed with him at nights and we attended church, but none of that mattered to him. We would always end up back where we started. When I found out I was pregnant with twins, I was devastated. I don't believe in abortion, but I wanted an abortion. Being pregnant pushed me back into his arms. A nightmare. I was so stressed out while carrying the babies. I didn't stop working because I didn't want to be home. I could barely sleep. He was so much like a kid, and required all of my attention regardless of how I felt. I was hurting a lot and he didn't care, "this is your fault", he would say. I was tired and fed up, I couldn't take it anymore. The last tragic event that took place could have cost me my life or my children's lives. I could have been taken away from my children for good. I was determined to take my life back and stand up for myself. By the time I got away from him, I was suffering bad. Deep depression, anxiety, bi-polar, you name it. My mental health was not good at all. I allowed someone to make me lose myself and forget who I was. I stopped eating, not sleeping, caring for two newborn babies, and sitting in the dark crying until I couldn't cry anymore. My hair was falling out, I was almost malnourished, but all I could do was pray. I got up one day and rebuked Satan in the name of Jesus! "Satan, you will not win!" I took my life back. I took my voice back, and decided not to cry anymore. I had to remember that God didn't bring me out of this turmoil to leave me, and I thanked God that he saved me.

Although, that meant I was left a single mother yet again. Raising four children all by myself, is a daily struggle and sometimes I cry and ask God "why". Then I think, well, why not me? The choices I made led me to where I am. Knowing God loves me despite all the choices I've made is what keeps me going. My father was the first man to break my heart, but it's my heavenly father that keeps me going, and allowing me to flourish.

Thank you Lord...

CHAPTER THIRTEEN

"Just Before Dawn"

Trina D. Wells

I dedicate this chapter to my "Shero"

~Talfrieda Michelle Covington~

TRAGEDY

The "tragedies of life" are a common place within our society today. People have very little respect for life and will take it without mutual consent. My family and I became victims of "tragedy" after the death of my sister. My mind tends to reminisce back to that horrific moment, that 5:00 a.m. phone call that changed our lives forever; a call that was made to my mother by one of the church mothers who lived a street over from my sister's home. She stated that a nearby neighbor had witnessed my sister's body laying outside her home covered in a puddle of blood.

After hanging up the phone, my mother immediately woke me, relaying the devastating news. We immediately got dressed and ran towards the door eagerly heading towards the car. I remember how we tried to pray on the way there, but the only words we managed to utter was "JESUS, JESUS, JESUS, JESUS" hoping to receive a different report when we got there.

Upon arrival, there were police officers, an ambulance and onlookers surrounding the premises. We knew the unthinkable had occurred at that point. Once we got out of the car we had to plow through the onlookers which felt like fighting through a sea of people. We finally made it towards the officers while noticing the yellow tape which signified a crime had been committed; that's when it all began to sink in. I remember my mother screaming to the officers as tears streamed down her face and with every word she spoke, I could feel the pain behind it, "Officer let me through - that's my daughter - please let me see my daughter." The officer informed her as kindly as he could while restraining her, "Ma'am, I am so sorry, but I cannot let you through.

You don't want to see her like this - this is now a crime scene." As I stood there in a daze looking at my sisters lifeless body covered under a white sheet and hearing my mother's screams penetrate the core of my soul, all I could do was run.

I know you thought "Forrest Gump" discovered the running method first, after losing JENNY the love of his life! But nope, it was me, **Trina D**… Please, laugh out loud; a little humor is good for the soul. I ran so fast, not knowing what direction to go, but I somehow ended up at the home of one of my dear friends that was close in proximity. When she finally opened the door, all I could do was fall inside her doorway. I felt like someone had punched me in my stomach and knocked the wind out of me. I will never forget trying to tell her what happened… the words would not form. I remember how she prayed for me which helped to calm me down quite a bit, making it easier to muster up the courage to share the devastating news with her.

I was in a state of shock, my soul was broken, Frieda was my only sister of my parents union and my "Shero." I wish you had the opportunity to meet her; she was so funny, loving, beautiful, caring, and mean ALL at the same time. She had a big heart, she was a great mother and loved her children very much. In fact she loved all people, it did not matter where they came from; she loved them unconditionally. Quite often, my mother would fuss, calling the people she desired to help "strays", even telling her that she could not help everybody. Although she did not have much, she ignored my mothers direction and helped those she could anyway. She was one who many enjoyed talking to about any & everything without feeling judged or criticized. When I think of her, these two scriptures sum up the quality of love "Frieda" shared towards others.

Ephesians 4:2: *"Be completely humble and gentle; be patient, bearing with one another in love,"* and *1 Peter 4:8: "Above all, love each other deeply, because love covers over a multitude of sins."*

I watched how "Frieda" fought through many challenges during her lifespan, even how she battled with **Epilepsy,** yet she persevered. I remember a time while in junior high. She fell on a piece of ice during a snowstorm and broke her jaw. She had to get it reset, wear rubber bands on her teeth for months and learn how to eat through a straw.

Yet she persevered and fought her way through it. That school year she fell behind on her schoolwork quite a bit resulting in repeating the 8th grade. Although she was disappointed within herself, my mother's pep talks managed to build up her confidence and once again, she preserved. Another fond memory was of a plaque my mother bought her that sat upon the mantle of our fireplace by the famous poet Walter Wintle that read:

"If you think you are beaten, you are

If you think you dare not, you don't,

If you like to win, but you think you can't It is almost certain you won't.

If you think you'll lose, you're lost For out of the world we find, Success begins with a fellow's will It's all in the state of mind.

If you think you are outclassed, you are You've got to think high to rise,

You've got to be sure of yourself before You can ever win a prize.

Life's battles don't always go To the stronger or faster man,

But soon or late the man who wins Is the man WHO THINKS HE CAN!"

I memorized that plague at age eight; it somehow became a frame of reference I tended to use, even to this very day. Although her future plans had been delayed by one year, she graduated from high school on God's time. I saw how she handled adversity despite how many times life hit her, she learned how to take it in stride and swung right back. She learned how to stay focused on the goal at-hand while ignoring the negative inner conversation and forging straight ahead. Looking back, I am not sure if she had any favorite scriptures, but I'd like to subscribe Phillipians 4:13 to her life, **"I Can do all things through Christ which strengthens me."** If she was here today she would say, "When life knocks you down, don't stay there on the ground, get back up and finish the round."

TRAUMA

Those of you that have experienced losing someone will agree that this statement is true: "You need people AFTER the funeral is over because that's when reality sets in." My sister's life was taken **"Just**

Before Dawn" at age 28, leaving behind two children, Kescha (5) and Kortney (2) at that time. We did not mentally prepare for the after affects this trauma would have on us, experiencing a wide range of physical and emotional reactions. I discovered that there is no "right" or "wrong" way to think, feel, or respond, so I stopped judging my own reactions and other family members as well. I later learned that **your responses are NORMAL reactions to ABNORMAL events.** Trauma can cause adverse effects to your mind, body and soul and create a wide-range of psychological symptoms that are hard to foresee. However, the best way to deal with trauma is to go to God first.

That is how my mother and I learned how to deal with the pain. Our faith in God, strength and our church family helped pull us through the hardship which led me on a deeper search. I found comfort in reading Psalms. David's writing seemed to resonate with me most as he knew a thing or two about having a "broken soul." A few of my favorite scriptures taught me how to deal with the blow of death… Psalms 23:3, "*He restoreth my soul; He leads me in the paths of righteousness For His name's sake*"; Psalms 42:1-7, "*As the deer panteth after the water brooks, so panteth my soul after thee, O God. 2 My soul thirsteth for God, for the living God: when shall I come and appear before God? 3 My tears have been my meat day and night, while they continually say unto me, Where is thy God? 4 When I remember these things, I pour out my soul in me: for I had gone with the multitude, I went with them to the house of God, with the voice of joy and praise, with a multitude that kept holy day. 5 Why art thou cast down, O my soul? and why art thou disquieted in me? hope thou in God: for I shall yet praise him for the help of his countenance. 6 O my God, my soul is cast down within me: therefore will I remember thee from the land of Jordan, and of the Hermonites, from the hill Mizar. 7 Deep calleth unto deep at the noise of thy waterspouts: all thy waves and thy billows are gone over me.*

Learning how to pour out your soul before the Lord is the precursor to your healing. People will try to make you think that we are to mask our emotions. Quite the contrary. Jesus did not mask His emotions after hearing Lazarus had died! We are not superhuman, we are to cry when things hurt us. This is apart of surrendering the hurt to the Lord. People told me to be strong for my mother and I did just that. I held it all in and went on to help plan the funeral. I picked out my sisters clothes, went to the funeral home, did her hair and make-up and gave the family tribute at the funeral. Because I had to be strong, I was doing exactly what I was told to do. It was not until after the funeral that I began to leak; my tears came up out of me from a place I did not know existed. Even though my tears were washing away some of the hurt, I somehow equated crying to being weak rather than being strong. But crying is not a sign of weakness nor does holding the pain inside mean that you're strong. It really means your running mentally instead of physically. When emotional pain is stored inside the body it will eventually catch up with you for the body will pay you back one day. I had to learn how to work through the hurt and press right into that pain without allowing others to judge me nor attempting to judge myself.

Dealing with Trauma is one thing, but fighting through grief is another factor of pain that can only be processed over time. Everytime I looked at my niece and nephew I felt their grief and wondered how this trauma would affect their future. No one can foresee the future so I had to gain comfort in knowing that they had a strong support system to help them process things as no one could fill that void of not having a mother, but God. Just as I learned how to surrender my hurt to the Lord, I also surrendered all my uncertain thoughts about my niece and nephew to the Lord as well. I had to believe that God was in control of their destiny; and my job was to make a positive contribution towards their well-being. When I look at them today as adults I see "Frieda" in both of them. Kescha has her radiant beauty, fire, spirit and personality. Kortney has her features: eyes, nose and mouth, her sense of humor and her mean streak. Foremost, my comfort is in knowing that "Frieda" is still living through her children and her legacy is still being written out through their lives each day.

I do wish sometimes that God could come down and hi-jack our pain so we could not feel it, but I am learning that even in our brokenness, God delights. Psalms 51:17 states, "***My sacrifice, O God, is a broken spirit; a broken and contrite heart you, God, will not despise.***

During those times, He teaches us lessons and how to grow, even from our pain. So I implore you, if you feel like CRYING, cry; if you feel like SCREAMING, scream and even if you feel like RUNNING, then Run Forest Run LOL! Being emotional does not mean that you are weak, it means you're surrendering your weakness to God, and His strength is made perfect in you. 2 Corinthians 12:9 states, "***And He said to me, "My grace is sufficient for you, for My strength is made*** *perfect in weakness." Therefore most gladly I will rather boast in my infirmities, that the power of Christ may rest upon me."*

Triumphant

Matthew 5:12 ***"Be joyful and triumphant, because your reward is great in the Heavens; for so were the Prophets before you persecuted."***

My sister, Talfrieda Michelle Covington is my "Shero." She overcame her challenges while living here on earth and will receive great rewards in Heaven. One week before my sister's horrific death, she dreamt about dying and shared the dream with my mother who encouraged her to dismiss it. Now, looking back on that situation, I believe God was preparing her to engage in the biggest battle of her life and used that dream to prepare her. Also, God knew that she would not win that battle, but to reign with Him meant she would win the WAR. As "Frieda" prepared for her departure, when Sunday came around, she took her children to church and she surrendered her life to the Lord. That final act of getting SAVED was a demonstration of her surrendering her Final Battle to the Lord.

All the battles she fought through and all the love she gave out to others was apart of her journey of living life to the fullest. Her prophetic dream was symbolic of Jesus in the Garden in Luke 22:42, ***"Father, if you are willing, take this cup from me, yet not my will, but yours be done."*** When she looked into her cup of suffering, it scared her, but instead of ignoring the signs like most people do, she yielded to the will of the Father, just like Jesus. You never know when God will announce your final battle in a dream or another form of communication, but I encourage you to leave here empty. Do not die full. Live your life on your own terms: Love hard, laugh a lot and be a blessing to as many as you can in accordance to the pattern that Jesus mandated.

"Frieda" fought the good fight and she finished the race strong. Timothy 4:7 states, ***"I have fought the good fight, I have finished the race, I have kept the faith."*** How will you finish? Who will you impact on the journey? Who will you love? Who will you be a blessing too?

Tragedy, Trauma & Triumphant are the three stages our family had to experience after our lost. We learned how to take advantage of all our possible resources in order to properly heal, which can only be done by walking with God one day at a time. A psychologist will tell you to lean into that pain even if it hurts you, a Pastor will tell you to pray and praise your way through because God is in tune with your grief. Our family had to apply both methods even when we felt like God was not moving fast enough and even when the 12 step plan to emotional recovery was not working. Our faith sustained us and pushed us through those most difficult times. Faith it, even when you cannot see your way, say it, for it will eventually lead you to a breakthrough.

When I observed how my mother rolled-up her sleeves and took care of my sister's children, raised them in the church, continued to go to work, encouraged others and built on what she had left, it was a remix of Faith, Resilience and Strength that we needed to see in order for our family to move forward. You can pick up the pieces of your life regardless of what you are left with. The leftover fragments are enough to remix and make great things happen again. Often when I think of my mother and how she got her "Fight Back" I think of the Biblical story of Naomi and Ruth; after Naomi lost her husband and her two sons, she had to go back and learn how to build on what she had left. Ruth was Naomi's bonus daughter God gave her to breathe new life into her and reclaim her destiny. Kescha and Kortney are my mother's bonus children and God used them to breathe new life back into her "broken soul". She got her second wind while raising them as she had more battles to fight and more rounds to win for the sake of "Frieda's" legacy. She is my "Shero" on a whole new level. God created women to be strong although they are considered the weaker vessel, but inside, they are pillars of strength.

I leave you with these encouraging words: You are stronger than you think you are, wiser than you give yourself credit for and a builder who has all the necessary tools, whether you believe it or not. You will WIN again, so get up, roll up your sleeves, lean into the hurt, breathe through every round & FINISH STRONG!

GIRL, Get Your Fight Back!

Made in the USA
Columbia, SC
05 January 2025